WHAT PEOPLE ARE SAYING ABOUT BOUNCE...

If you have ever been in a dark place where discouragement, depression, and anxiety were your constant companions, this book is for you. When we walk through "the valley of the shadow of death," we need the Shepherd to show us the "green pastures" and the "still waters." On this 60-day journey, Donna Gibbs, a seasoned counselor, will help you draw upon the power of Christ to bring you into the sunlight again.

Gary Chapman, Ph.D.
Author of *The Five Love Languages*

People everywhere are desperate for help, hope, and deep encouragement. Resilience—the "bounce back" effect—is a crucial factor at the heart of this timely devotional, which is anchored in messages of healing and wholeness. AACC member and experienced Christian counselor, Donna Gibbs, offers strength for the journey as we battle the challenges and stress of our modern world. Her book is a gift to help us all live free in Christ.

Tim Clinton
President of American Association of Christian Counselors
Julie Clinton
President of Extraordinary Women

With gospel-centered truth accompanied by practical steps forward, *Bounce* is so much more than a book. This is your daily meeting with a counselor who has one goal: to send you straight into the healing words and presence of your Wonderful Counselor. Donna's words are biblical, full of grace and truly come from the trenches of pursuing resilience herself. Whether your goal is to gain or gain back your confidence in Christ, this is a powerful tool that will help you (and those around you!) get there.

Michelle Myers
Co-founder and co-author of *She Works His Way*
Author of the *Conversational Commentary* series

"Life is Hard, but Faith is Firm." My longtime friend and counselor has "words fitly spoken" in this great devotional. This is "wisdom literature" for life. I love encouraging people, but I battle worry, anxiety, and stress. Donna's chapters provide me with God's healing touch and perspective. She's one of Jesus' best physicians of the soul. Enjoy each paragraph as you embrace wholeness. To put it succinctly: These devos help The Swan!

Dennis Swanberg
Americas Minister of Encouragement
DennisSwanberg.com

Bounce is a 60-day devotional that will bring you great encouragement as you face challenges and discouragement. It will give you the kind of resilience that inspires and motivates you to run to God, not from Him. Christian counselor, Donna Gibbs, will take you on this journey through messages of comfort and hope that will bring you closer to the Lord while helping you to be "transformed by the renewal of your mind" (Romans 12:2).

> Dr. Bruce Frank
> Lead Pastor of Biltmore Church
> Asheville, North Carolina

All of us face life's normal challenges, stresses, and setbacks, and many of us endure far more serious trauma and devastating loss. Our experience of God's love, power, and presence is the key to overcoming heartaches. In *Bounce*, Donna Gibbs gives us a powerful and practical way to point people to the grace of Christ for mental health support in the face of pain and suffering. Donna's empathy and compassion, mixed with her experience of over 25 years as a Christian counselor, make her a trusted guide for our journey toward resilience.

> Jennifer Ellers, MA
> Co-author of *The First 48 Hours: Spiritual Caregivers as First Responders*
> Senior Director of AACC's Advancement, Special Projects, and
> Church Engagement

The older I get, the more I want to cut through the fluff and get to real talk. In this devotional, Donna does a great job of this by being honest about the struggles of life, providing insights gained through the fires of experience, and sharing perspective and hope from God's Word.

> Kevin Wimbish, LMFT
> Co-owner, Summit Wellness Centers, PLLC

Bounce

A 60-Day Devotional to
Jump-Start Your Resilience

DONNA GIBBS

*Dedicated to those around the globe who
have faced challenges and discouragement,
and are eager to bounce back.*

CONTENTS

INTRODUCTION

When life is hard, you may feel like you've been thrown to the ground. Common mental health symptoms like depression and anxiety have increased as we've suffered from the pandemic and its aftereffects, political polarization, misinformation, and economic uncertainty, in addition to the normal stresses and strains of family life and work. Today, you may be desperate to bounce back, but you don't know where to start.

I get it.

I am you.

I too have been thrown to the ground. I too have faced discouragement . . . even desperation. I too have faced situations that threatened my mental health. And I had to find a way to survive the weight of my seemingly hopeless circumstances.

Let me explain just one of those circumstances . . .

I'll never forget the day when my physician stood by my hospital bed and solemnly delivered the news of a very bad diagnosis. You know, the kind of news that punches you in the gut . . . that takes your breath . . . that temporarily stops time.

Here's what I heard: "Your best-case scenario is that you will be here for a long time. Not weeks, but months. If your length of stay is any less than that, then it means things didn't end well. With that said, you are going to have to put into place, *for yourself,* every tool you've ever used as a counselor. We can't afford for you to get depressed. That will only make things worse."

Shortly after I heard this sobering news and my doctor's desperate prayer for God's help, he turned and left the room. That conversation was in the early days of my three-months-long stay in the hospital. My condition was serious, and we both knew it. We also knew just how crucial my mental, emotional, and spiritual health would be—because I was entering the physical battle of my life.

I took my physician's challenge seriously, and I did exactly what he prescribed. I also did exactly what he prescribed for my mental health. *As instructed, I used every tool that I had ever recommended to another person.* Some days the fight was harder than others. Some days I struggled more than others. Some days I cried. Some days I was fearful. Some days I was angry. Most days I was lonely. But I refused to allow depression to take hold of me. *It wasn't easy.* But by the grace of God, I was victorious!

Please hear me:

I know what it's like to be up against a wall.

To be afraid.

To feel that what you're going through isn't fair.

To face an unknown future.

To feel trapped in physical and emotional pain.

To wrestle with God.

I'm not going to share anything in this devotional that I haven't already found to be successful in more than twenty-five years as a professional Christian counselor, working with thousands of clients who have faced unthinkable tragedy, heartache, and emotional distress. And I'm not going to share anything in this devotional that I haven't already successfully used during that grueling physical battle, and the many battles I've faced since then.

Life can be hard. We all experience seasons of suffering, loss, rejection, betrayal, pain, and disappointment. Maybe you're living through one of those darker, colder seasons right now.

You're hurting.

But you aren't alone.

Perhaps it's too late to avoid the pain, but it's never too late to cope well.

And it's never too soon to start bouncing back.

Speaking of bouncing back . . . Anytime I think of the word *resilience*, I always think of a bouncy ball. I know, it seems so elementary, but I've always loved a simple and concrete visual, and a rubber ball is the perfect illustration of the kind of bounce back you and I are longing for. So, let's just think for a moment about what happens when you throw a ball to the ground.

Though we can't see it with the naked eye, when a ball hits the ground, it compresses slightly, and then it springs forward with power, restores its shape, and bounces back up. In fact, the harder you throw it down, the higher it bounces. It seems to defy gravity.

If you throw it down at an angle, it's not just a bounce back. That's a bounce forward!

I long for that kind of resilience. To bounce back from a challenging season, and eventually come out stronger than I started. *I bet you long for a bounce forward too!*

But is it possible to bounce forward from heartache? From depression? From anxiety? From rejection? From betrayal? From abuse? From unthinkable tragedy? From failure? From _________? (You fill in the blank.)

I don't know your story, but I know this: If you've been slammed to the ground recently, you almost certainly wonder if there is any bounce left in you.

You wonder how it could be possible that you could come back stronger than ever. It may be hard to imagine that you could be resilient.

But I know that your resilience *is* possible because I know the God who authors resilience. I have seen evidence of His hand in facilitating a defiant bounce forward in the lives of thousands of individuals within the quiet walls of my office.

Nothing is impossible with Him!

The passage of Scripture that gave me the analogy of a bouncy ball is the same passage that I find myself meditating on in each season of struggle of my life. God spoke through the prophet Isaiah, "Remember not the former things, nor consider the things of old. Behold, I am doing a new thing; now it springs forth, do you not perceive it? I will make a way in the wilderness and rivers in the desert" (Isaiah 43:18-19).

Wow! That powerful word is worthy of reading again and again.

Maybe you've just been stuck for a short season, or maybe you've been stuck for years. In either case, please realize that you don't have to stay stuck anymore. God desires to do something *new* in your life, but you must look for it. You must reposition your focus from your past and current circumstances so you can gaze on God's miraculous intervention to release you to live fully in wisdom, strength, and joy.

Though God is more than capable of miraculous deliverance, His healing is more often *through a process* which follows His timeline, and not ours. He often leads us to walk *through* our pain, rather than around it or away from it. In other words, *bouncing forward is a journey*, rather than a one-time event.

Will you trust Him to walk with you through this journey? Will you trust Him with your suffering? With your mental anguish?

Will you trust Him to give you resilience?

It's time to allow a "new thing" to "spring forth" and add some bounce to your life!

Since God is the author of resilience, we're going to let Him take the lead in this journey. We're going to examine His Word and ask Him to examine our hearts. We're going to rely on His tools for our minds, our bodies, and our souls—not the flawed and ineffective coping skills that might be keeping us stuck and creating unnecessary, additional suffering.

This is resilience . . . God's way!

So, if you're desperate to bounce forward, but you don't know where to start . . .

Start here! This devotional is for you! This is a 60-day journey designed to jump-start your resilience. You'll read just one short devotional a day. You'll notice that each day's entry is brief. That's because concentration is a challenge when we feel anxious or depressed. Each day's devotion is specifically organized to facilitate your physical, emotional, mental, and spiritual growth, and to provide practical tools for resilience. Every day of the journey provides validation, education, instruction, encouragement, a point to ponder (a task or a tool for the day that develops resilience), a single verse for your meditation, my prayer for you, and a section where I invite you to think and pray about what you've just read. Be sure to journal your victories throughout the journey and invite a few friends along who could also benefit from some resilience. We're better together!

Now, it's time to jump-start your bounce forward!

Thanks for joining me on the journey!

DAY 1 NORMALIZE THE PAIN

Until 2020, we were generally well-insulated from pain in America.

So insulated that it's often hard for us to remember that pain is a normal part of the human condition.

The truth is that occasional symptoms of sadness, weariness, anxiety, and feeling overwhelmed *are* a normal part of the human experience.

Unfortunately, due to our attempts to insulate ourselves from pain, we shame ourselves when we experience any kind of distress. This shame causes us to think we are different from everyone else and keeps us stuck in our pain.

Wise King Solomon normalized the existence of personal struggle. He wrote, "For everything there is a season, and a time for every matter under heaven" (Ecclesiastes 3:1).

The Apostle Paul was featured in Luke's account of the early church in Acts, and Paul wrote many of the letters to the churches. Despite his incredible strengths, he also transparently acknowledged a chronic, unidentified struggle: "... a thorn was given me in the flesh, a messenger of Satan to harass me, to keep me from becoming conceited. Three times I pleaded with the Lord about this, that it should leave me. But he said to me, 'My grace is sufficient for you, for my power is made perfect in weakness'" (2 Corinthians 12: 7-9).

King Solomon was not protected from pain.

Paul was not protected from pain.

Neither am I.

And neither are you.

When we embrace the reality that trials and suffering are normal on this side of heaven, we are less inclined to feel we must hide our pain with a fabricated smile.

PONDER THAT!

Today, normalize the universal experience of suffering and struggle. Reflect on respected historical, biblical leaders who wrestled in ways similar to yours. Consider acquaintances, neighbors, or mentors who have walked through difficult trials. Consider friends or family members who have endured painful challenges. Allow their humanity to remind you of yours, and their experience of pain to normalize yours. Permit yourself to be honest about your tough season.

VERSES OF HOPE

For everything there is a season, and a time for every matter under heaven: a time to be born, and a time to die; a time to plant, and a time to pluck up what is planted; a time to kill, and a time to heal; a time to break down, and a time to build up; a time to weep, and a time to laugh; a time to mourn, and a time to dance; a time to cast away stones, and a time to gather stones together; a time to embrace, and a time to refrain from embracing; a time to seek, and a time to lose; a time to keep, and a time to cast away; a time to tear, and a time to sew; a time to keep silence, and a time to speak; a time to love, and a time to hate; a time for war, and a time for peace. —*Ecclesiastes 3:1-8*

MY PRAYER FOR YOU TODAY

God, I pray for my friends who are reading this devotion today.

Remind them that suffering is a normal part of the human condition. Validate their season of pain. Remind them of other heroes of the Scriptures who experienced significant distress, hardship, betrayal, physical ailments, and attacks—heroes who sometimes felt defeated . . . who experienced doubt, discouragement, depression . . . who were sometimes afraid, mad, or deeply saddened . . . who experienced trauma. Thank you for the lives of people like David, Esther, Job, Peter, Hannah, and Paul. People just like us who faced unthinkable difficulties and endured through challenging seasons. People who demonstrated great faith, while also acknowledging great distress.

Thank you especially for Jesus, who ran toward His distress, so that we would have a place to run in ours.

Father, encourage my friends with hope today, as you remind them that this is a season. There will be better, more pleasant seasons to come. Soon, a smile will become easier. They will breathe lighter again. The heaviness will be lifted. Their face will brighten once more. We thank you for the hope of Jesus and our eventual, eternal season of glory with You. Until then, help us to manage our painful seasons faithfully, and prepare us for a bounce forward on this side of Heaven.

THINK AND PRAY

What is your typical response to painful seasons in your life?

What strategies have you used to insulate yourself from emotional pain? (Minimizing the pain, excusing people who hurt you, distracting yourself so you don't feel, etc.)

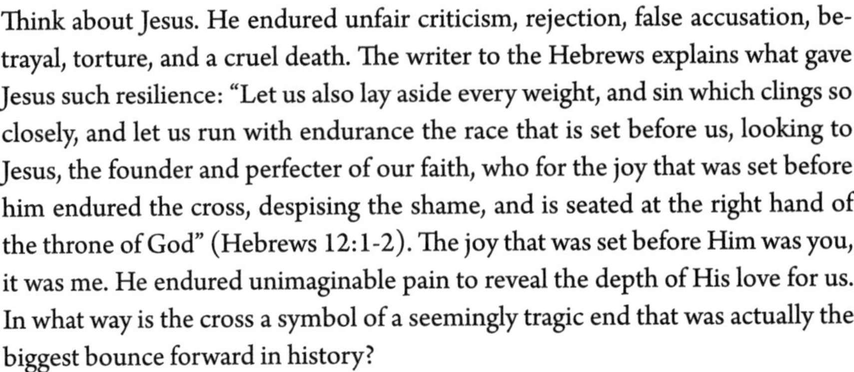

DAY 1

Think about Jesus. He endured unfair criticism, rejection, false accusation, betrayal, torture, and a cruel death. The writer to the Hebrews explains what gave Jesus such resilience: "Let us also lay aside every weight, and sin which clings so closely, and let us run with endurance the race that is set before us, looking to Jesus, the founder and perfecter of our faith, who for the joy that was set before him endured the cross, despising the shame, and is seated at the right hand of the throne of God" (Hebrews 12:1-2). The joy that was set before Him was you, it was me. He endured unimaginable pain to reveal the depth of His love for us. In what way is the cross a symbol of a seemingly tragic end that was actually the biggest bounce forward in history?

Review the Verses of Hope. Remind yourself of the temporary nature of your current season. List or highlight the future seasons that you are most hopeful about.

Make my prayer your own.

Our minds are prone to wander.

Unfortunately, when our minds wander into the future, rarely do they wander within the confines of truth.

We tend to wander toward the catastrophic.

We meditate on the possibilities of the future with eyes on the worst-case scenario. **Our bodies keep the score of our fears, with physical symptoms that prove our angst and invite unnecessary suffering.**

Our brains and bodies assume that our catastrophic thoughts are based on our current reality. They don't realize that the threat is self-generated by our thoughts wandering and catastrophizing. Too often, those thoughts trigger a cascade of emotional and physical symptoms into our *present* that are painful to feel and even harder to manage.

So our heart palpitates.

Our shoulders tighten.

Our head aches.

Our stomach roils.

We break out in a sweat.

We're prone to anxiety.

God knew our creative, brilliant, problem-solving minds would be vulnerable to catastrophic thinking. That's why He gave us guidelines for managing our thoughts.

He advised that we focus on the troubles of *today*, while avoiding excessive problem-solving regarding *tomorrow*.

PONDER THAT!

I know . . . It's so hard to keep focused on today! We need mental guardrails that protect our minds from wandering into the catastrophic. Today, strengthen the muscles of your mental health by managing your thoughts and placing mental guardrails to keep you in today, preventing you from getting stuck on thoughts that wander into tomorrow. When you catch yourself in a catastrophic thought about the future, visualize that thought bouncing off the guardrails in your mind, never allowed to hold you captive. Or, remember your "helmet of salvation," and visualize a catastrophic thought bouncing off like a small pebble against a steel helmet.

VERSE OF HOPE

"Therefore do not be anxious about tomorrow,
For tomorrow will be anxious for itself.
Sufficient for the day is its own trouble."
—*Matthew 6:34*

MY PRAYER FOR YOU TODAY

God, I pray for my friends who are reading
this devotion today.

Their minds are prone to wander into the catastrophic
possibilities of the future. They know what it's like to be anxious,
and they wrestle with managing that emotional
and physical response.

Father, give them mental guardrails. And show them when and
how to use these invisible boundaries for their minds.

Guide them in attending to the concerns of today, and protect
them from unnecessary worry regarding tomorrow.

Thank you for the sunrise and sunset that defines our day and
reminds us to be in this moment with You.

Not shamefully looking back.

Not obsessively looking ahead.

But in this moment.

Right now, with You.

Defeat any stronghold of fear, and reveal any other triggers that
are fueling their anxiety, as You continue to equip
them for resilience.

THINK AND PRAY

What are the most frequent catastrophic thoughts about "what might be" that cause you angst?

What internal resistance do you experience when you practice using your mental guardrails?

How can you balance responsible readiness for the future with being grounded in today?

Make my prayer your own.

DAY 3 THESE THINGS I REMEMBER

The psalmist was depressed.

The Psalms are reflections of the writers' cries, their raw emotions, their frustrations and anger, their impatience with God to relieve their pain. For instance, "My tears have been my food day and night" (42:3).

Can you relate? Are you struggling to eat? Do you find yourself crying through the day? Crying through the night?

Discouraged? Overwhelmed?

The people who wrote the poetry of the Bible could relate. But they also had a great tool: "These things I remember" (42:4).

The writer of this psalm allowed his tears to shift his focus to memories of God's faithfulness. He reflected on times when he'd seen the evidence of God's hand in previous situations. He reflected on what he had witnessed in other seasons regarding the character of God.

The psalmist allowed his pain to pivot his eyes to the origin of his hope.

Remembering truth prevented him from being stuck in his depressive state, and it positioned him to bounce forward.

PONDER THAT!

If you need to cry out to God today, feel free. The psalmist did, and you can too. God created your body to release tears, and He can handle your raw emotion and pain. But allow those tears to prompt you to remember God's faithfulness, evidence of His character in your life, and experiences of victory. These memories are evidence of the hope that applies to today's pain.

VERSE OF HOPE

Why are you cast down, O my soul,
    and why are you in turmoil within me?
Hope in God; for I shall again praise him,
    my salvation.
—*Psalm 42:5*

MY PRAYER FOR YOU TODAY

God, I pray for my friends who are reading this devotion today.

Remind them that You created them with the capacity to cry.

Remind them that You track all their sorrows. Not a single tear goes unnoticed.

Remind them how much You loved the psalmist's heart, and how eagerly You welcome them as they bring their raw emotions to Your throne today.

Help them today in the midst of their discouragement.

Help them remember Your faithfulness, Your goodness, and Your power.

Remind them of the times in their lives when You drew near. When they felt Your presence. When You intervened. When You delivered. When You saved.

Remind them of the desperate times in their past when they saw evidence of Your hand.

Remind them.

Help them to never forget.

I pray that You'll use their memory to help them bounce forward.

THINK AND PRAY

How do you relate to the psalmist's emotional turmoil?

When have you experienced God's faithfulness? (List all the situations you can remember.)

What emotions do you feel as you remember? How does remembering those situations help you today?

Make my prayer your own.

HIS STEADFAST LOVE

David often called out for God's mercy.

Mercy during times of emotional pain and despair.

Mercy during times of shame and regret.

Mercy against the threats of his enemies.

Mercy in physical pain.

David was aware of his deep need for God's grace and help.

David was also aware of God's great love for him. "God will send out his steadfast love and his faithfulness!" (Psalm 57:3) David interpreted God's love in ways that we often overlook because our culture uses the word "love" to apply to so many superficial aspects of life.

David understood that God's love was not a superficial or fleeting emotion. **David understood that God's love is a** covenant love. Dependable, faithful, and everlasting. A stubborn love, without conditions.

With this understanding, David managed some of his most painful moments by meditating on God's enormous, radical, covenant love. He found his refuge and his relief in the assurance that God would not and could not forsake him, due to the covenant nature of His love.

Perhaps like David, you are in emotional or physical pain today, and you are aware of your need for God's mercy, grace, and help.

Call on Him.

Cry out to Him.

If you are His child, God's covenant, faithful love is already yours, and He will send out His love, meeting you at your point of pain.

PONDER THAT!

Allow God's radical love to wrap you. Meditate on His *covenant* of love, like a blanket that covers you. Stay there. Focus on your breathing right now, as you allow yourself to breathe the truth of God's extravagant love deep into your being. Accept His love with every breath you take. Allow the assurance of His covenant love to challenge the doubts that hold you captive.

VERSE OF HOPE

He will send from heaven and save me; he will put to shame him who tramples on me. God will send out his steadfast love and his faithfulness! —*Psalm 57:3*

MY PRAYER FOR YOU TODAY

God, I pray for my friends who are reading this devotion today.

I pray You will prepare their hearts to embrace Your love in a way they've never known before. Be gentle as You wrap them in Your unfamiliar covenant of love.

Be gracious, as their finite minds find it hard to imagine Your love could be that extravagant. That radical. That faithful. That dependable. That beautiful.

It seems overgenerous. Too good to be true.

Hold their doubts far away, Father, and allow them to feel the love of a perfect daddy. A capacity for love they've never experienced before.

Help them interpret Your love just as David did, without the superficial definitions of the word we use today. Give them freedom in Your love and the courage to embrace the bounce forward that You have lovingly designed for them.

THINK AND PRAY

What do you think is the difference between how you have understood God's love and how David understood His love?

What does it feel like to be approached by a God who has a radical, covenant love for you? How are you welcoming this? How are you fearful of it . . . of Him?

Make my prayer your own.

 # CONNECTED

You search for excuses to say "no" to invitations. You rarely answer your phone. You don't respond to text messages.

You long for relationships, and yet you also dread relationships. You find it hard to engage in small talk when you are struggling. So you often sit alone. Retreating into the familiar quiet and darkness of discouragement.

But the silence is deafening, and the loneliness is suffocating.

Discouragement thrusts us powerfully toward isolation, and the loneliness found there drives us even further into a pit of despair. **Seclusion is a trap. A quick trip to depression.**

Solitary confinement is used in our prison system as an incentive to control behavior, but there are federal laws restricting how long a prisoner can remain in forced isolation. Why? Because this method of punishment is considered by some to be psychologically torturous, leaving inmates vulnerable to depression, anxiety, and even psychosis.

So when we isolate for days, weeks, and even months, we're incarcerating ourselves, and treating ourselves as if we were a dangerous and uncooperative prisoner. But we weren't created to live a disconnected life.

If you are downcast today, you are probably inclined to withdraw from those you know and love. But isolation never helps. Isolation only provides more opportunity for the darkness to close in.

Isolation will hijack your encouragement.

Consider Paul, who was often afflicted by physical and emotional difficulties. He was also the most relational hero in the Bible. Much of what we know of Paul is the result of his writing to a group of believers. Despite the forced isolation he often experienced because of imprisonment, he went out of his way to connect with others. When he could visit them face to face, he did. When he couldn't, he wrote them, and he received letters from them. He spoke very openly about his love for people, and he drew encouragement from his connections with other believers.

PONDER THAT!

Consider the people God has put in your life. You weren't designed to live in isolation. People need you. And you need people. Today, call, text, write, or visit a friend. Intentionally resist the urge to isolate yourself.

VERSE OF HOPE

But since we were torn away from you, brothers, for a short time, in person not in heart, we endeavored the more eagerly and with great desire to see you face to face. —*1 Thessalonians 2:17*

MY PRAYER FOR YOU TODAY

God, I pray for my friends who are reading this devotion today.

Sometimes they isolate. Not because they want to be alone, but because it feels overwhelming to even consider being with others. Sometimes they just feel drawn to a hibernation that never refreshes. That never keeps its promise to be better than community.

God, remind them that You created them for community, and that their brains and bodies respond to the presence of meaningful relationships.

They need others.

Others need them.

Give them the desire, and the courage, to step out today. To respond to a text message today. To return a phone call today. To invite a friend to coffee. To attend that Bible study they've heard about. To make plans today to go to church this weekend.

Father, I pray that You will use others to pierce through the darkness of isolation. I pray the spiral of despair will be halted, and they will bounce forward because they were brave enough to have a conversation with an old or new friend today!

THINK AND PRAY

When do you experience the temptation to withdraw? Why does isolation seem so attractive?

What psychological effects do you generally experience following a period of isolation?

What symptoms of isolation are you noticing right now?

Make my prayer your own.

 # WALKING WOUNDED

I know you hurt.

Some days seem unbearable. Like you can barely function. Most days, you just feel that you're one of the walking wounded.

If you've experienced any kind of trauma, you may feel chronically broken. You may wrestle with uninvited flashbacks. You may even feel that your experiences have severely complicated your life and that your chances for the life that you've always wanted are ruined.

Joseph may have once thought that way. Sold into captivity by his own brothers. Imprisoned and forgotten. Accused of things he didn't do. But his story didn't end there. God raised him up to be a leader in Egypt. Joseph used his suffering and his strengths to save two nations from famine. (See Genesis 37, 39—50.)

Esther may have thought her life was ruined. Orphaned. Taken captive as a teen through what was the equivalent of a modern-day sex trafficking scheme. Yet God raised her up to be an instrument in saving an entire nation, using her suffering and strengths "for such a time as this" (Esther 4:14).

The Scriptures are full of broken people who have endured significant trauma. You won't have to look hard to find them. They probably experienced symptoms that you can relate to: Disturbing memories. Nightmares. Trouble sleeping. Crying spells. Isolating. Avoiding conversations about the past. Irritability and anger. Difficulty concentrating. Anxiety. Depression. Sometimes feeling numb. Other times, looking for a *way* to feel numb. These are normal reactions to abnormal situations. Experiences and wounds that should never have been.

Over and over again in the Scriptures, we see evidence that **God often uses broken and wounded people, and He demonstrates His power to move them through their trauma to bounce them forward in ways that are purposeful, productive, and healing.**

He never wastes our pain!

My friend, your pain doesn't have to end with pain. Your symptoms can be calmed, and your brokenness can propel you to purpose and healing.

PONDER THAT!

Today, give yourself permission to imagine that your open wounds can become healed scars, and your pain can be transformed into purpose. Submit your suffering and your strengths to God, and allow Him to initiate the transformation process of beautiful resilience. Yes, you are wounded. But you are walking.

VERSE OF HOPE

"For if you keep silent at this time, relief and deliverance will rise for the Jews from another place, but you and your father's house will perish. And who knows whether you have not come to the kingdom for such a time as this?" —*Esther 4:14*

MY PRAYER FOR YOU TODAY

God, I pray for my friends who are reading this devotion today.

Some of my friends know trauma only too well. They connect to the symptoms we've just listed. And to the stories of Joseph and Esther.

They too have been wounded, and they sometimes feel that they are limping through life because of the pains of the past.

Jesus, I pray that You would remind them of Your trauma. Remind them of Your physical suffering. Your humiliation. Your torture. The public spectacle. The misunderstandings. Your sacrifice.

You know trauma.

But You also heal trauma.

Father, meet them at their point of pain, gently soothe their wounds, remind them of their worth, and begin moving them out of their trauma and into their healing. Give them a glimpse of what life can be on the other side of their pain.

THINK AND PRAY

How are wounds of your past impacting your present?

What symptoms of trauma are you noticing today?

Who is God putting on your heart to reach out to today?

Make my prayer your own.

  # FALSE GUILT

Guilt.

It's an enemy to mental health.

It's so easy to get stuck there. We all have regrets. Things we wished we had done differently, or not at all. Mistakes we've made. Sins we've committed. Words we wish we could take back. Appalling actions. If you have continuing remorse over your past, you may be struggling with guilt. The good news is that guilt, fueled by conviction of the Holy Spirit, can productively compel us to repent and experience God's limitless forgiveness, which paves the way to freedom and resilience.

But quite often, guilt is a tool of the enemy. Past missteps haunt us. The memories crush us, beating us over the head with reminders of how pathetic we are. Inviting shame and feelings of unworthiness. Keeping us stuck. Preventing our bounce, because our feelings of unworthiness are so convincing that they keep us from experiencing God's forgiveness.

On the other hand, you may be blaming yourself today for something that you already repented for, and God has forgiven you . . . days ago, weeks ago, or maybe years ago. This feeling is *condemnation*, and it's not coming from God.

It's false guilt. It's keeping you stuck and preventing your bounce!

Or you may be blaming yourself today for something that God has never tapped you on the shoulder and whispered, "That was wrong." Something was wrong, all right, but it was something harmful that someone else said or did. You've suffered from guilt for years over something that wasn't your fault, because it was easier to blame yourself than to acknowledge what really happened. You didn't want to face the reality that someone hurt you and didn't care. It was easier to be a sponge, soaking up all the blame. This continued self-blame is condemnation, and it is not coming from God. *It wasn't your fault.* There was no sin. You didn't make a mistake. There was no error on your part.

False guilt is always authored by the accuser, Satan. The condemnation you feel from false guilt is not from God, and it's the source of many mental health symptoms.

PONDER THAT!

Be honest with yourself. If you carry guilt about unconfessed sin, run to the Father in repentance. That guilt that you are feeling is the conviction of the Holy Spirit, a productive alert to sin. Jesus is waiting with grace. His arms are wide open, and He's ready to convince you that the cross paid for that sin . . . and every sin. There's no benefit to carrying that guilt. It will only prevent your bounce forward. There is freedom in forgiveness.

Or, if you are oppressed by Satan's accusation and condemnation, due either to false guilt or nagging, previously forgiven regrets, today is a day to release the oppression. Agree with God today about your situation and write yourself a letter of release, as if it were written from God to you. Let Him remind you of His deep well of forgiveness and love, and drink deeply. Keep the letter in your wallet—it's ammunition for the next time you hear the whisper of false guilt.

VERSE OF HOPE

There is therefore now no condemnation for those who are in Christ Jesus. —*Romans 8:1*

MY PRAYER FOR YOU TODAY

God, I pray for my friends who are reading this devotion today.

Guilt has been a great manipulator and a tool of the enemy. It has effectively kept them stuck in shame and condemnation.

I pray You would give them discernment regarding any productive conviction related to unconfessed sin, in contrast to false guilt that only harasses, condemns, and keeps them stuck.

Father, remove any blinders that deceive them from seeing truth.

Give them freedom from the bondage of false guilt. Lift that heavy weight so they can bounce forward.

THINK AND PRAY

How would you define or describe false guilt? What has been its role in keeping you stuck?

What are your concerns about releasing the condemnation you feel?

What reservations do you have about bouncing forward?

Make my prayer your own.

DAY 8   GREAT EXPECTATIONS

Frustration. Anger. Resentment. Sadness. Disappointment. These are the normal emotional responses of unmet expectations.

Some realistic, but unmet expectations are relatively benign, and just require a conversation and an adjustment. These are nonessential expectations. Things like when a friend is routinely late for coffee, or when someone takes your assigned parking space at work. These unmet expectations are noticeable, but are more like a pebble in the shoe, not a boulder that crushes you.

Realistic, unmet expectations that are connected to basic needs are far more challenging. For instance, it's realistic to expect a parent to protect. A spouse to be faithful. A friend to be loyal. For your body to be respected. When these expectations are unmet, it's nothing like a pebble in a shoe. These unmet expectations are a boulder that creates trauma and leaves us disillusioned and grief-stricken. To heal, we must acknowledge the hurt, both to ourselves and at least one safe person. But we also must establish physical and emotional safety. *Unmet realistic expectations give us a strong signal that adjustments must be made.* We must change our expectations, and modify our lives, or we will be wounded repetitively from the same, stubborn expectation that's unmet time and time again.

But sometimes, *unmet* expectations are born out of *unrealistic* expectations. Things like expecting that a relationship will always be conflict-free, or that a spouse can read us and know what we need without being asked, or that a child will always obey. Perhaps it's a more personal expectation. Things like expecting that we will never experience failure, health issues, wrinkles, or symptoms of depression or anxiety.

Unrealistic expectations create tension in relationships, often placing impossible demands on loved ones. These expectations result in anger, criticism, division, and discontent. Unrealistic expectations that are more personal in nature create a drive for perfectionism and make us vulnerable to shame, anxiety, and depression.

Our culture makes it extremely difficult to maintain realistic expectations. It's imperative that we do some evaluating of expectations in an effort to maintain our mental health and stability.

Be honest today about your *grieved realistic expectations,* your *unrealistic expectations,* and the potential need to *adjust expectations* so that you are resting in truth and regulating your emotions without undue complications. Why? **Because unrealistic expectations will rob you of joy and compromise your mental health!**

PONDER THAT!

Consider the root of any negative emotional responses you've recently experienced. Do you notice the presence of any unmet expectations (regarding relationships, work, health, etc.)? If so, then you are grieving. It is possible that you also have some unrealistic expectations. Invite God to reveal any expectations that set your relationships up for failure and create an emotional rollercoaster that's jeopardizing your stability. Ask Him to reveal who or what might be fueling your unrealistic expectations (social media, group of friends, etc.)

VERSE OF HOPE

So we do not lose heart. Though our outer self is wasting away, our inner self is being renewed day by day. —*2 Corinthians 4:16*

MY PRAYER FOR YOU TODAY

God, I pray for my friends who are reading this devotion today.

Today's devotion has triggered memories and provided insights for them. I pray You will use what they are understanding about expectations to bring freedom and resilience. To allow them to become unstuck.

Guide them toward any necessary adjustments in expectations. Give them courage as they seek to respond to Your leading.

Thank you, Father, for Your faithfulness in meeting our expectations. You are forever with us, never to forsake. Refresh my friends with reminders that You are who You say You are, and that You will always complete what You start. May Your faithfulness be grounding and comforting as they move ahead through their struggles and do the hard work on their journey.

THINK AND PRAY

What insights is God revealing about the role of unmet expectations in your life?

In what ways are you grieving those unmet expectations?

In what ways are you frustrated by unrealistic expectations (from yourself or others)?

Make my prayer your own.

 FROM PAIN TO PERSPECTIVE

Are you silent in your struggle today? So fearful of losing control of your emotions that you aggressively avoid acknowledging or discussing something challenging in your life?

In a very emotional psalm, David explained the damage caused by suppressing his emotions: "I was mute and silent; I held my peace to no avail, and my distress grew worse. My heart became hot within me. As I mused, the fire burned" (Psalm 39:2-3).

Like David, are you guarding your tongue with such hypervigilance that you deny and suppress your emotions? Do you notice the effects of anger burning "hot" within you?

As believers, we often seek to monitor our mouth. (And for good reason, as we've all experienced the sins of a tongue unleashed.) **But if we aren't processing raw emotions in the safety of our communication with God, anger will well up, much like putting a match to kindling and watching the fire grow.**

David could sympathize. He stuffed his negative emotions, waiting for peace to come. But it didn't. His effort to deflate his distress backfired. Instead of pouring water on his fire, his stuffing only ignited his fury. His "distress grew worse" (Psalm 39:2)

But notice how David checked himself. He didn't stay stuck. Nor did he remain silent. He unmuzzled and interrupted his distress with a simple but honest conversation with God. **He regulated his emotions by using his voice; his words directed his heart to submission and rest.** David pivoted. **God traded his pain for perspective** as David was taken to a fresh place of awareness related to the brevity of life.

PONDER THAT!

Do you notice anger welling up in your spirit? Gripping your body with tension? Are you exhausted from trying so hard to prevent an outburst? Are you, like David, stuffing and muzzled? It's time to break the silence. Talk with God right now. Like David, speak honestly of your struggle. Don't continue to stuff your painful feelings. Acknowledge your specific thoughts and emotions. Then, trust Him to redirect your thoughts and regulate your emotions. Notice as He brings the kind of perspective that allows your anger to take a seat and His truth to take the lead, as He faithfully guides you in how to respond effectively to your situation.

VERSES OF HOPE

I was mute and silent;
I held my peace to no avail,
    and my distress grew worse.
    My heart became hot within me.
    As I mused, the fire burned.
—*Psalm 39:2 3*

MY PRAYER FOR YOU TODAY

God, I pray for my friends who are reading this devotion today.

God, remind them that You are safe. That You can handle their mess, and their messy emotions. And that You are waiting to listen.

I pray that the silence is breaking, right now. I pray that they will find peace once again as they speak out loud, using their tongue to process their emotions, just as David did.

May my friends find safety in seeking You, just as David did years ago:

"And now, O Lord, for what do I wait?
My hope is in you. . . .

Hear my prayer, O Lord,
and give ear to my cry;
hold not your peace at my tears!" (Psalm 39:7, 12)

I pray the distress will melt away as they pour out their hearts to You. I pray they will no more futilely suppress what You already know is inside them. And I pray that, much like David, You will refresh them with an eternal perspective that distances them from their anger and boosts them in their bounce.

THINK AND PRAY

Do you tend to suppress painful emotions, such as anger, fear, and hurt? What is the perceived payoff of suppressing them?

How has suppressing your emotions caused even more anger, fear, and hurt?

Today's challenge involves breaking the silence. Follow David's example and have a raw conversation with God. During and after it, how are you feeling?

Make my prayer your own.

 # PILOTING ANGER

Anger is such a tough emotion! Unfortunately, when we're struggling, we're bound to experience the full range of anger and its obvious sidekicks: irritability, frustration, sarcasm, and outbursts. When anger is unrelieved or hurt ungrieved, we may experience less obvious symptoms like anxiety, depression, or self-pity. And when anger camps out in our heart, we eventually also experience bitterness.

God has created us with the capacity to experience every human emotion, including anger. Anger is a normal and healthy response to injustice. But we struggle to handle this emotion well, so it sits, grows, and consumes us. Anger in and of itself is not a sin, *but it is the emotion in which we are most likely to sin,* because rarely is anger managed in a godly manner. As a result, our anger tends to create a mess, and its consequences often invite even more struggle into our lives.

Additional struggle that we can't afford.

Today, if you're feeling the pang of anger, remember that it is a secondary emotion. You're almost certainly feeling something else that makes you feel more vulnerable (such as fear, insecurity, reminders of past pain, etc.). Anger is the subconscious mask that is seemingly more protective than the cascade of other vulnerable emotions that might also be present in your mind and heart.

Today, focus on following God's instruction to *slow* our anger. To *slow* our speech. I know, it's hard, but it's possible. Think of it like slowing down in a sharp curve to avoid a dangerous crash. It's okay to be angry, but let's be honest about this often-deceptive emotion, and **let's make sure that we pilot our emotions, rather than allowing our emotions to pilot us.**

PONDER THAT!

Today, choose to be the pilot of your anger, but first, you need to be able to identify it. Is your anger plainly evident in resentment, sarcasm, and blame, or does it live in the less obvious realm of depression and self-pity? If you are angry today, give yourself a productive time-out. In that time, consider the vulnerable primary emotions that are underneath the surface your anger. Name those emotions and their triggers (such as reminders of past hurts, a demanding spouse, unrealistic expectations at work, a distressing health diagnosis, etc.). Sit with those emotions. Be honest with yourself about your vulnerability. Then brainstorm specific and practical ways your anger can be used productively rather than allowing it to become destructive. Determine your steps before you re-engage with those around you, and thank God that He has given you a healthy, productive way to express your anger.

VERSES OF HOPE

Know this, my beloved brothers: let every person be quick to hear, slow to speak, slow to anger; for the anger of man does not produce the righteousness of God. —*James 1:19-20*

MY PRAYER FOR YOU TODAY

God, I pray for my friends who are reading this devotion today.

They are angry. And You know their reasons.

You have created them with the capacity to feel this intimidating emotion, so lead them through it in a way that honors You.

Give them the pause they need for the frustrations they will encounter today. Help them distinguish between healthy anger, a normal response to injustice, and unhealthy anger which is the result of ungrieved emotional wounds from the past. Give them awareness of any negative thoughts that are falsely guiding their anger, and provide wisdom to navigate a righteous emotional response to injustice.

Guide them as they slow down and use this fiery emotion in a manner that brings You glory, with appropriate boundaries for their responses to their triggers. Protect them from being deceived. Protect them from a sinful response to anger.

Father, You created the emotion of anger with a purpose—as powerful fuel when it is needed. Today, I pray You redirect their anger toward the things that are keeping them stuck.

Remove any blinders or distractions and allow their anger to be
a godly force that You use to jumpstart their resilience!

THINK AND PRAY

Is your anger the kind that's more obvious or more hidden?

Who are the people and what are the recurring events that trigger your anger?

How would you define and describe "healthy anger"?

Make my prayer your own.

DAY 11 HEALING THE BROKEN HEART

Your heart hurts. The emotional heaviness is physically tangible. You feel it in every way. Every moment of every day. It's impossible not to notice it.

You've always heard the phrase, "a broken heart." You've probably even heard people talk about *takotsubo cardiomyopathy*, or broken-heart syndrome. It seemed unreal that someone could suffer heart complications because of emotional distress. You thought it was fake news.

But today, those reports seem more believable. Every part of your physical body now hurts . . . because your soul is injured.

You may be cautiously encouraged by the words of the psalmist, "The Lord is near to the brokenhearted and saves the crushed in spirit" (Psalm 34:18). You are hesitant to let God draw too near. You're anxious and ask, "What if . . .?" Anticipating the next potential blow creates a wall, so you refuse to allow Him who is drawing near to get closer. Pushing Him far away is easier.

You want to run toward Him, and you make some halting steps. But then you run away from Him instead. And then you do it all over again. It's a vicious cycle. Because pain . . . is painful.

But what if you stopped running in either direction? Neither toward nor away from Him. What if you just stop right where you are . . . and just breathe? Breathe and be still. And let Him come to you. **Let Him be near.** Let Him attend to your pain. Let Him touch your crushed spirit. Let Him gently and safely console you.

There, in His presence, you'll discover that God doesn't just simply draw near. He's not merely a passerby who notices your pain and stands there in your surroundings, watching as you ache and suffer. There, in His presence, you'll also discover that He "binds up" your wounds. Only our Creator would know that our hearts could break from a soul wound and need to be bound in times of pain. **God knows your vulnerability and your broken heart.** He is the first responder who is running to the scene. Running toward your pain. Positioned, available, and capable of delicately and tightly holding your broken heart.

Let your Rescuer come to your aid. Let Him bind your wound. Let Him touch your crushed spirit. Let Him give you hope again!

PONDER THAT!

Today, be still. Breathe. You are in pain, and your first responder is on His way. Notice as God gently draws near. He'll be the first on the scene if you will allow Him. Let Him be your physical, emotional, spiritual, and psychological first aid. He knows you. He understands you. He sees your pain. He is offering His presence. Trust Him to soothe your broken heart and restore your crushed spirit.

VERSE OF HOPE

He heals the brokenhearted and binds up their wounds. —*Psalm 147:3*

MY PRAYER FOR YOU TODAY

God, I pray for my friends who are reading this devotion today.

You know them. You understand them. And You see their pain. You see their crushed spirit. You even see every physical ache and pain that their broken heart causes them to feel.

You are drawing near, but You're not just drawing near to get a closer look. You're not just there out of curiosity or for Your entertainment.

You're there to bind their wounds!

Thank you, Father, for noticing!

Thank You for being a safe first responder! Thank You for Your gentle and loving aid.

I pray that my friends can be still, right now. That they can let You be near, right now.

I pray they will allow You to bind their wounds and launch their bounce!

THINK AND PRAY

What breaks your heart today?

Where does the emotional pain show up to affect your body?

What are your concerns about God drawing near? What are your hopes?

Make my prayer your own.

 # WHEN THE BURDEN IS BIG

Do you carry a heavy burden today?

Are you burdened by a wound or a loss that weighs heavy on your heart and mind? Are the circumstances of life threatening your mental health?

You're not alone.

While your specific burden is unique to you, almost everyone throughout history has experienced a desperate moment. If you are despairing today, you will resonate with Esther's distress. The story tells us that Esther discovered an unthinkable plot—an evil scheme that placed the entire Jewish nation in grave danger. Her people would perish without intervention.

Esther faced a genuinely desperate situation. As the queen, she was the only Jew who had any chance of preventing the slaughter, but this slight chance of victory came at the very real risk of her life.

Can you imagine the intrusive and destructive thoughts she may have battled during the days approaching her visit to the king? She may have suffered from an onslaught of unusually intense and confusing emotions. She probably experienced some acute mental health symptoms.

Psychological distress would have been a normal response to her abnormal situation, not an indication of her typical mental wellbeing. But Esther's coping response to this burden is a strategy worth adopting. In her distress, she gathered a group of trusted people and initiated a united plea to God. She called for her people to fast with her and on her behalf.

Desperate situations inevitably find us. You've either had one, you're in one now, or you're going to have one sometime in the future. It will be a situation that changes the trajectory of your life and threatens your mental and emotional stability. Fasting (denying something physical for a spiritual gain) is an appropriate response to desperation.

PONDER THAT!

If you are facing a desperate situation today, consider using Esther's response as a model. Gather the trusted people in your life, choose a method of fasting, and focus on fervent prayer. The bigger your burden, the more stabilizing will be God's spiritual filling.

VERSE OF HOPE

"Go, gather all the Jews to be found in Susa, and hold a fast on my behalf, and do not eat or drink for three days, night or day. I and my young women will also fast as you do. Then I will go to the king, though it is against the law, and if I perish, I perish." —*Esther 4:16*

MY PRAYER FOR YOU TODAY

God, I pray for my friends who are reading this devotion today.

Some of them are in a desperate situation. They face something that could change life as they've always known it.

Remind them that they aren't alone.

No one shares their exact story, but everyone has a story.

Inspire them with Esther's story.

Encourage them to follow Esther's model, guide them as they gather their trusted people, and humble them to seek Your face. Fill them as they fast, and give them courage to face the unknown.

Remind them that resilience is less about the ending, and more about the forward-focused journey.

THINK AND PRAY

What is your desperate situation today?

How are you coping under the weight of uncertainty?

How is God specifically leading you to follow Esther's example? What difference will it make?

Make my prayer your own.

 # NEW MERCIES

Mornings can be unpredictable. Some mornings you wake encouraged and hopeful. And some mornings you're struck with a wave of sadness that weighs you down. On those mornings, you feel empty and struggle to just get out of bed.

We've all had mornings like that.

By God's grace, the sun comes up every morning. It's the symbol of a new day. A daily reminder that the dawn changes everything. For the Israelites, the dawn was the time God provided fresh manna. It was just what they needed to sustain them.

Nothing more.

Nothing less.

And nothing like they'd ever had before.

For us, the dawn is accompanied by fresh mercies. **Like manna, a sufficient portion, renewed each day.**

This morning, when your feet hit the floor and you meet the new challenges of the day, know that God also meets you with new mercies.

God's mercies were renewed with the first light of day, and they will be refreshed every day of your existence.

So this morning, remind today's struggles that you have today's mercies.

PONDER THAT!

If you woke this morning encouraged and hopeful, then take a moment to thank God for this gift. If you woke this morning with physical, mental, emotional, and spiritual exhaustion, then go to God right now and ask for some daily manna. God will give you all that you need. Nothing more. Nothing less.

No matter how you wake today, get up. Make up your bed. Shower, get dressed, and remind today's struggles that God's mercies are new today.

VERSES OF HOPE

The steadfast love of the Lord never ceases; his mercies never come to an end; they are new every morning; great is your faithfulness. "The Lord is my portion," says my soul, "Therefore I will hope in him." —*Lamentations 3:22-24*

MY PRAYER FOR YOU TODAY

God, I pray for my friends who are reading this devotion today.

Some of my friends woke this morning refreshed and hopeful, ready to embrace the day.

God, thank You for that gift.

Some of my friends are still in the bed, wrestling with the sheets because they are wrestling with their emotions. They woke with heaviness, but they're trying, they're studying this devotion, and they're asking You for help. God, You promised to faithfully meet them there with Your new mercies. Remind them of Your faithfulness to the Israelites—and that You are the same God now that You were then. You have the power and creativity to use whatever refreshing method You would like, and I praise You with confidence that Your mercy for them today will be all the manna they need for the struggles they face.

Give them the bounce today to get up out of bed. To begin moving. To shower. To make their bed. To eat a nutritious meal. To be productive. And to embrace their purpose for being alive today.

God, let Your mercy fall like fresh manna, nourishing them as they bounce forward today!

THINK AND PRAY

How do you relate to the Israelites, who were entirely dependent on God to provide the strength, energy, nourishment, and hope they needed each day?

How are you experiencing God's mercies right now?

What is the biggest concern you have for the day ahead? What does it mean to receive God's mercy for this struggle?

Make my prayer your own.

Family. The word almost always produces an emotional response. Some respond by feeling safe, supported, and hopeful. If this is you, be grateful for your family because you have experienced love and acceptance there. When you struggle with the world, you long to return home. You know that everything will be better when you can go back to the safety of those who love you.

But if you just cringe when you hear the word *family*, it's because you've had some past struggles with your home life. Some frustrations. Maybe some hurt. Maybe even real trauma. Family is not where you run *to* when life is hard. Instead, family is what you escape *from*.

Family dynamics can be so hard. *Every* family system has its complexities, and each member has a role. Your heritage may be "messed up" and marked by deception, drama, and disappointment. Or maybe it's characterized by abuse and abandonment.

Though some family systems are admittedly healthier than others, there is no perfectly healthy family dynamic. **Every family is made of sinful individuals, with each generation leaving dysfunctional patterns that influence the next.**

If your family dynamics are the greatest threat to your mental health, triggering feelings of unworthiness, fear, anger, and shame, then a visit back to the Gospels is appropriate. At first glance, the first chapter of the book of Matthew looks like a boring narrative covering the names of forty-two generations. But a deeper dive reveals that this is not just any group of people. *This is the lineage of Jesus.* These are generations of people from various upbringings, some of whom were stricken by poverty and struggle, and others who were engaged in all kinds of twisted and devious shenanigans. For instance, though Solomon was born after the adulterous affair of David and Bathsheba, David and Solomon still had significant roles in the lineage of Jesus, and Bathsheba is still identified in this lineage as being the wife of Uriah.

Why? Because God sees our identity . . . beyond our messes.

This is the genealogy of Jesus; a reminder that God forgives sin and can use *all* challenging family dynamics for His glory!

PONDER THAT!

Today, consider the dynamics of your immediate family, and go back a generation to consider the dynamics of your family of origin. Pray that God would allow you to see your family system from His perspective, and rest in God's power and grace to use a broken heritage to bring about the birth of Jesus. This means He can use the sins and wounds in your background to make you wiser, stronger, and more compassionate toward others who are affected by their past.

VERSES OF HOPE

. . . and Jacob the father of Joseph the husband of Mary, of whom Jesus was born, who is called Christ. So all the generations from Abraham to David were fourteen generations, and from David to the deportation to Babylon fourteen generations, and from the deportation to Babylon to the Christ fourteen generations. —*Matthew 1:16-17*

MY PRAYER FOR YOU TODAY

God, I pray for my friends who are reading this devotion today.

Thank You, God, for placing the lineage of Jesus in Your Word, validating the presence of dysfunction in the family of every life. Even a perfectly holy life.

I am grateful that some of my friends find rest when they run to family. Thank you for giving them that refuge with people they love.

I pray You will minister to my friends who have experienced unthinkable trauma from those who failed them. I pray that You will heal them, redefine their identity in You, and remind them that You can use every family pattern for Your glory! Give them wisdom and courage to become a family that heals.

I pray that when they see the lineage of Jesus, You will give them relief from shame and a deep hope that You can use even the worst that we endure to deepen our faith and produce character in us. Free them to embrace the bounce that You have waiting!

THINK AND PRAY

What words would you use to describe the individuals and the patterns of inter-actions within your immediate family?

What about the family in which you grew up?

How does your family dynamic (past and present) impact your emotional well-being?

Make my prayer your own.

*If today's devotion about family triggers a painful trauma response, reach out to someone who can pray with you and support you through your healing. You are not alone!

Favoritism. That word may sting. If the word favoritism causes your stomach to turn, it's because someone has "played favorites," and it has affected your life in a powerfully painful way.

Perhaps you've been judged because of things out of your control. A mental illness. Your skin color. Your family of origin. An intellectual or physical disability. You can relate to the example referenced in the second chapter of James: the poor man who was asked to sit on the floor while the rich man was offered a seat of honor.

You can relate, because you've also been unfairly judged while others received favor. You know what it's like to be treated as if you were broken, unwanted, or unworthy.

If you wrestle with physical or mental health challenges, financial hurdles, childhood trauma, or cultural differences, you may have been misunderstood, and you've felt that others would have preferred you to figuratively "sit on the floor" instead of enjoying community. The bias, judgment, or rejection by others has been profoundly wounding, possibly causing you to doubt your worth, and leading to feelings of shame.

If you've experienced this deep hurt, I'm so sorry.

Truly sorry.

But you need to know:

That wasn't Jesus who looked down on you.

That wasn't Jesus who misunderstood you.

My friend, despite any hurtful experiences of favoritism, know that you are highly favored. The God of the Universe loves you so much. He created you, and He was perfectly pleased with His design of you! Your strengths, your flaws.

He chose you.

PONDER THAT!

Today, you may be remembering some painful interactions in your past. It's okay to acknowledge that it was painful to have been treated unfairly. Today, hold together those old memories and emotions, along with truth about God's lavish favor and His firm opposition to favoritism. God hates partiality. He sees the unfairness that has wounded you. From preschool to today, nothing went unnoticed. Allow Him to hold you, to gently nurture you. Allow Him to affirm your worth.

God also sees where your favoritism has wounded others. Allow Him to give you a new perspective about the hurts you may have caused. Experience the depth of His forgiveness, and let His love for you increase your empathy towards others that you have unfairly judged.

No matter the offender, God stands in opposition to the transgression of favoritism, but He rewards mercy with mercy.

VERSES OF HOPE

If you really fulfill the royal law according to the Scripture, "You shall love your neighbor as yourself," you are doing well. But if you show partiality, you are committing sin and are convicted by the law as transgressors. . . . So speak and so act as those who are to be judged under the law of liberty. For judgment is without mercy to one who has shown no mercy. Mercy triumphs over judgment.
—James 2: 8-9, 12-13

MY PRAYER FOR YOU TODAY

God, I pray for my friends who are reading this devotion today.

I pray You will speak healing truth that is a salve to the wounds that favoritism has created. Remind them that You see all that is unseen. Nothing was unnoticed. Every tear accounted for.

You have a word for every wound. Give them ears to hear Your healing whispers.

I pray You will validate their emotional responses and shield them from bitterness. Give them a heart of mercy despite the past hurt.

Father, reveal any area in which they have wounded others with judgment or favoritism. Expand their compassion and empathy toward others as they confess truth and accept Your mercy. Reward their mercy with mercy, because mercy triumphs over judgment.

Bless their courage in acknowledging their pain and seeking You for healing. I pray they will be encouraged as they see and experience Your kindness and strength.

THINK AND PRAY

What would you say to encourage the poor man described in James 2:1-3? Write out your words.

Now, speak those words of favor back to yourself.

How did you experience being the recipient of your favor?

Make my prayer your own.

 # INSECURITIES

If you're like most people, you struggle. Sometimes you wrestle with thoughts that you aren't good enough. That you don't measure up.

You aren't attractive enough . . .

or successful enough . . .

or popular enough . . .

or spiritual enough.

You're not a good enough spouse, or leader, or employee, or parent.

The "not good enoughs" can be exasperating! Put those distracting thoughts to the side for just a moment, because I want you to be able to hear an important truth: **Mental stability hinges on the accuracy and consistency of our thoughts.** But when we are wrestling with insecurity, our thoughts are anything but truthful and stable.

If you have ever struggled with feeling that you don't measure up, your emotions have suffered a beating. Your spiritual life and your relationships have suffered. **The enemy wants that insecurity to touch *every* part of your life.**

Every.

Part.

It's time you take your life back. *But you'll have to leave those insecurities behind.* And you won't be able to relinquish those destructive and deceitful conclusions until you embrace the truth . . . about God, about yourself, and about your situation.

PONDER THAT!

Today, consider the various ways you have been robbed by insecurities. How have they impacted your mental health? Your relationships? Your decisions? Your career? If insecurities have robbed you, it's okay to be angry. Allow your anger to propel you toward truth.

VERSE OF HOPE

But the Lord said to Samuel, "Do not look on his appearance or on the height of his stature, because I have rejected him. For the Lord sees not as man sees: man looks on the outward appearance, but the Lord looks on the heart." —*1 Samuel 16:7*

MY PRAYER FOR YOU TODAY

God, I pray for my friends who are reading this devotion today.

Expose any lies they are believing that cause them to shrink in shame.

Lies that are threatening their mental health and impacting their relationships.

Reveal the truth about who You are. And who they are in You.

Refresh them with knowledge of Your radical, sacrificial, unconditional love.

Impress on them a heart knowledge—not just an intellectual knowledge, but a knowledge that sees beyond the superficial and discerns the truth.

Protect them from the accusations of the enemy, who seeks to destroy them by creating a falsehood regarding their significance.

Thank You for being the Rescuer of their identity.

THINK AND PRAY

What are the most frequent, degrading thoughts you have about yourself? Write them out so that you are more easily able to discern truth. "I am . . ."

How are these condemning, destructive thoughts fueling your insecurity?

Take a moment to hold those destructive thoughts beside today's Verse of Hope. Meditate there, allowing God's truth to speak to your destructive thoughts. How does this truth shift your *thinking*?

How does this truth shift your *emotions*?

Make my prayer your own.

 # WISDOM IN MEEKNESS

Jealousy is an invisible force. And we're all vulnerable. Maybe you're feeling the pang of jealousy today. You see others making bank with their jobs, but you're struggling to make ends meet. You see others spending time with grandkids, but you are estranged. You see others in a happy marriage, but you are grieving a divorce. You see others laughing, but you're having to work on a fake smile.

Do you see the theme? **"You see others . . ." and then you compare and focus on your inadequacy.** Every day, we're inundated with data that triggers thoughts of inadequacy. Our negative thoughts then trigger the emotional response of jealousy. And jealousy feels awful! So awful that we naturally seek to do something to stifle the discomfort. Selfish ambition is the natural—and destructive—result.

We strive in our own efforts to be seen.

To be known.

To be approved.

To be respected.

To be celebrated.

But it's never enough. Though unseen and often undetected, our selfish ambition fuels even deeper insecurities, threatens our mental health, and becomes toxic. **But wisdom is birthed in "meekness."**

Meekness is not a toxic insecurity; it's a healthy posture that acknowledges the chosen and radically loved position of a believer in Christ, as well as the "pure . . . peaceable . . . gentle . . . sincere" and powerfully effective wisdom given by God!

Meekness builds up . . . and stabilizes. Wisdom allows us to pivot from thoughts of inadequacy to truth about our worth and our circumstances. As a result, wisdom stifles jealousy and stabilizes emotions far better than selfish ambition ever could, and it births godly ambition that brings glory to the One who holds all wisdom and understanding.

Wow! That certainly takes the performance trap down a notch! And when we remove performance as the source of our identity, we gain freedom and mental health.

PONDER THAT!

Today, consider the theme of *"You see others…"* Be aware of comparisons that trigger thoughts of inadequacy. Notice how jealousy is often triggered in your life. Right now, guide yourself to meekly pivot from thoughts of inadequacy to truth about your worth and circumstance.

VERSES OF HOPE

For where jealousy and selfish ambition exist, there will be disorder and every vile practice. But the wisdom from above is first pure, then peaceable, gentle, open to reason, full of mercy and good fruits, impartial and sincere. —*James 3:16-17*

MY PRAYER FOR YOU TODAY

God, I pray for my friends who are reading this devotion today.

We've all experienced jealousy, because we've all let our eyes entice us to compare. We've all been vulnerable to selfish ambition.

Because ultimately, we all want to be seen, heard, and experienced as someone who has value, yet we seek these things from the wrong sources—our performance, popularity, and possessions. But these eventually leave us empty and confused. We find real love, security, and purpose only in the grace of God.

God, I pray that You would expose any stronghold of jealousy or self-ambition. Reveal any "disorder" or "vile practice" in the lives of my friends that is rooted in jealousy.

Give my friends wisdom as they consider who or what has their eye and is the object of comparison, feeding feelings of inadequacy.

Invite them into a healthy posture of meekness and repentance, where wisdom is found.

Free them from the captivity of comparison and selfish ambition. Unleash the chains of jealousy that have been keeping them stuck and preventing their bounce!

THINK AND PRAY

What's the connection between comparison and jealousy? In what way do you see evidence of selfish ambition in your thoughts and daydreams? What problems is this creating?

How is jealousy creating disorder in your life?

Think back to when you started this journey: In what ways are you moving forward in your bounce? (Don't be bashful here. Acknowledging your victories is not prideful. It's giving honor and glory to the One who is orchestrating your victories and providing you with all the ingredients you need to get unstuck).

Make my prayer your own.

HIJACKED BY BITTERNESS

We've all been wounded. A perceived injustice. Something that cost us more than we ever wanted to pay financially, relationally, emotionally, or otherwise.

And it wasn't our fault.

I've been hurt. You've been hurt. Perhaps you have been the victim of an unthinkable betrayal. Or a violation against your body. **When the person who offended you could never pay you back for the hurt, injustice leaves you vulnerable to bitterness.**

Sometimes we hold on to unforgiveness because we think that releasing someone condones what they did. Sometimes we hold on to the hurt because it allows us to feel protected from future harm. We're afraid of becoming soft or weak. Sometimes we hold on to bitterness because it seems that it is the only way our offender can ever be punished. And sometimes we treasure our bitterness because it gives us two things we desperately want: an adrenaline rush and an identity as "the one who was wronged."

But if you are holding on to past hurts today, *you* are the one being punished. **And your bitterness could be jeopardizing your mental health.** Unresolved anger holds us captive, turns us inward, hijacks our thoughts, leaves us vulnerable to depression, and can even leave us more vulnerable to physical diseases. Resentment seemed so protective . . . but it's not protective at all. In fact, *unforgiveness is a dangerous "friend" that seemingly shields us but instead wounds us.*

The truth? **Unforgiveness and bitterness take over where our offender stopped, and wounds us when our offender no longer can.**

Forgiveness is not unsafe, irresponsible, or enabling. It is simply a movement of your heart.

God may never call you to reconciliation. But He will always call you to forgiveness because He cares about you, and ultimately wants to protect you from the unrelenting harm of bitterness that keeps you stuck and sabotages your bounce forward.

PONDER THAT!

Time will not heal your wound. *Time alone has never healed a wound.* That's why there are lots of old, bitter people. Don't be robbed of another day. Releasing a bitter wound starts by recognizing the *unearned gift* of forgiveness that you have been offered through the sacrificial death of Jesus. Forgiveness is a process. And that process begins with one step as simple (and as hard) as extending a spoken or unspoken release to another sinful (or even evil) person who can never earn your forgiveness. It is a gift that you give yourself; a gift that can facilitate your process out of the clutches of bitterness and into the journey of your bounce!

***Forgiving someone who caused trauma can be a complex process. If you realize that bitterness has hijacked your mental health, reach out today for help. Find a friend, mentor, counselor, or pastor who can walk alongside you and facilitate your process of healing.**

VERSE OF HOPE

But God shows his love for us in that while we were still sinners, Christ died for us. —*Romans 5:8*

MY PRAYER FOR YOU TODAY

God, I pray for my friends who are reading this devotion today.

I pray they will experience Your presence amid their pain. Remind them today that You see their hurt. Their pain. Their trauma. Give them the ability to envision life without the tension of bitterness related to past hurts. To imagine living without the weight of the unresolved anger. Allow them to imagine the freedom that comes when they can hand that pain off to You.

Remind them of the gift of Your forgiveness. Refresh them as they reflect on Your radical love. And embolden them with the courage to release the pain that is tormenting them. Out of the overflow of Your forgiveness, I pray You will give them the grace to forgive those who haven't earned (or asked for) their forgiveness. I pray You will give them confidence to move forward with that first step of forgiveness. And that with each trigger that comes in the days and months ahead, You will give them the memory and assurance of their choice to forgive.

I pray that You draw near them as they go through this vulnerable process,

move out of bitterness, become unstuck, and bounce forward.

THINK AND PRAY

Write one word or draw a symbol that represents a specific wound that's unresolved and has left you vulnerable to bitterness.

I know you've been hurt. But how has unforgiveness also harmed you?

Forgiveness is both a decision and a process. What wounds are you ready to release right now? What will it look like to grieve the losses and heal the broken parts as the process continues?

Make my prayer your own.

  # COPING SKILLS

How are you coping? Are you keeping your head above water? Or do you feel like you're drowning? Today, it's time to consider how we're coping and what tools we are depending on. It's an important focus because resilience is entirely dependent on our ability to cope, and some tough seasons of life require more coping skills than others.

But not all coping skills are equal. Some are healthy and useful. Others are downright destructive.

In the presence of depression, anxiety, or other more complex mental health symptoms, our temptation is to rely on coping skills that numb our pain. *Some coping skills are highly effective at numbing our pain but horrible at facilitating growth through our pain.*

The problem? **If you just numb pain, you sabotage your ability to grow in wisdom, strength, perseverance, and maturity.**

Coping skills that numb pain stunt our growth because they circumvent God's ability to strengthen us through our suffering.

Alcohol is just one example of a coping skill that is highly effective for numbing pain, but it's also a depressant and is addictive, *causing our development through suffering to be arrested.* It's a poor coping skill.

This is the very reason God cautioned us to rely on the Holy Spirit instead of alcohol—because He desires our growth and comfort through the valleys of life, and He never wants our resilience to be restricted.

PONDER THAT!

Consider your coping skills today. Are you relying on alcohol, sex, shopping, social media, or other numbing agents? These coping skills may be temporarily effective in facilitating your escape, but they may also dig another pit of unintended dependence. Consider what these destructive coping skills might be costing you. Instead, nurture healthy coping skills (like prayer, journaling, speaking with a friend, exercise, etc.). Allow these tools to effectively address, rather than numb, your pain.

VERSE OF HOPE

And do not get drunk with wine, for that is debauchery, but be filled with the Spirit. —*Ephesians 5:18*

MY PRAYER FOR YOU TODAY

God, I pray for my friends who are reading this devotion today.

I pray You will equip them today with the tools they need to manage the trials they face. Remove any blinders related to coping skills that could ruin their lives. Convict them of any area where they are numbing rather than relying on You.

Give them courage to face their problems in the raw, without using any form of coping that sabotages their bounce and arrests their development.

Fill them with Your Holy Spirit. Let Your presence be the coping skill that fills, refreshes, encourages, instructs, and equips.

You are the author of resilience.

THINK AND PRAY

Consider how you are coping. Are you keeping your head above water? Or do you feel like you are drowning?

Take inventory of your coping skills, especially those that numb or distract. What tools do you most often rely on when you're discouraged?

How has your bounce been arrested by poor coping skills?

Make my prayer your own.

 # STRONGHOLD

You never intended it to be this way. No one ever does.

Stronghold. It sounds like such a complicated, spiritual word! But what is a stronghold? A stronghold is simply anything that has a strong . . . hold. Anything that hinders us spiritually, emotionally, or relationally. A stronghold can be big or small. It can be a temptation, a disorder, an addiction, or a hang-up. (The list is almost endless, including drug addiction, lust, emotional connection with someone not your spouse, eating disorder, overspending, pride, cutting, compulsive eating, social media addiction, pornography, stealing, lying, unforgiveness, gossip, self-loathing, occult involvement, etc.)

Sometimes a stronghold begins with a single act of rebellion that becomes an unintended pattern. Other times, a stronghold begins as a coping skill to distract or numb during a tough season of life, and then unintentionally grows into a more significant attachment. Something that eventually has control of us.

A stronghold is generally something we believe we must hide. It's a tool the enemy presents as an enticing substitute for attachment or dependence on God. Sometimes it's such a familiar part of our lives that we don't even realize it's a stronghold.

No one ever sets out to be controlled by a stronghold.

Take a moment to examine your heart. Is there something in your life that stands between you and God? That affects your personal relationships? That impacts the way you see yourself? That causes you shame? That tempts you to hide? That controls you more than you'd like to admit?

David understood. He was secretly controlled by lust for another man's wife. It nearly destroyed every aspect of his life, but when Nathan confronted him, David responded humbly in confession, "I have sinned against the Lord" (2 Samuel 12:13). David's bold turn from his stronghold changed the trajectory of his future. Strongholds persist because they're based on the illusion that you can't do anything about them. If you are oppressed by a stronghold, you don't have to live there. You *can* live without it. Just as David broke free, you can too.

PONDER THAT!

If you can relate to my description of wrestling with a stronghold that you never intended to have, give that stronghold a name today. Call it what it is. No sugarcoating. No minimizing. No excusing. *Write down* the name of your stronghold.

Contemplate what the stronghold has cost you. What has it taken from you? How has it robbed you? What would your life be without it? How would relationships be different? Your finances? Your emotional stability? Your job? Your parenting? Your health? Your spiritual life? Your family?

Write down your answers to these questions.

Notice your emotional response as you contemplate these tough questions. Let those negative emotions fuel your resolve to be free, and then put the enemy in his place. You are an heir with Christ. You have access to the same power that raised Christ from the dead, but the enemy is causing you to remain a slave to an unworthy master! Have no more of it! Proclaim *God* to be your stronghold when you find yourself in the grips of a *false* stronghold.

If you feel overcome by a stronghold, don't give up! Use your authority in Jesus! Reach out for help and commit to walking away from the destructive effects of this unintended attachment. Replace the stronghold with God's grace, truth, love, and power.

VERSE OF HOPE

The Lord is my light and my salvation;
whom shall I fear?
    The Lord is the stronghold of my life;
    of whom shall I be afraid?
—*Psalm 27:1*

MY PRAYER FOR YOU TODAY

God, I pray for my friends who are reading this devotion today.

Some of them are oppressed by a stronghold that they never imagined would have a role in their lives. It costs them far more than they ever intended to pay.

Father, You are their light. You are illuminating their way out.

You are their salvation. You paid everything so that they could fearlessly face their stronghold.

Remind them that You are their stronghold, and with You in their grip, they don't have to be afraid of this journey.

Release them from the chains of any toxic dependence so they can continue to bounce forward today!

THINK AND PRAY

Consider any stronghold in your life (past or present). Did it start as an act of rebellion that led to a destructive pattern? Or as a numbing coping skill that resulted in an unhealthy dependence?

What is God speaking to you about any current toxic dependence in your life?

If you are battling a stronghold right now, who can you reach out to? What difference will it make?

Make my prayer your own.

 # AVOIDING AN IMPLOSION

One of my colleagues only reads books that were written by deceased authors. I joke with him about it, and his reply is always, "Authors who are alive still have the chance to mess up." Ouch! That's true, isn't it? All of us can name someone we've admired who later disappointed us. Their music, their writings, their company, their ministry . . . forever tainted by their implosion.

It's not that God can't forgive. It's that we can't forget. And reputations are forever contaminated by a fall. The truth is that we too can "mess up." **As long as we still have breath, we all still have the option of wrecking our lives.**

I've done a lot of damage control over the years. All too often, my role has been crisis intervention after a life, marriage, family, or ministry has been wrecked. A controversial social media post. A DUI. An affair. A financial scandal. A mental health crash. People who are far smarter than me have invited destruction into their lives without ever intending to send an invitation. Anyone can self-destruct. No one is immune. In fact, *our sinful nature is naturally bent toward an implosion.* **But I've learned some of my most treasured and humbling lessons from wise people who suffered a collapse they never intended.** The awareness that anyone can fall keeps me on my toes.

This topic is especially important right now because the last few years have been dominated by a pandemic, political tensions, social isolation, and a mental health crisis. These stressors have deepened the very vulnerabilities that can lead to an implosion. We are all in a particularly vulnerable time and space. Our prevention of self-imposed ruin is dependent on the awareness of our weaknesses and the coping skills that we utilize to manage our inevitable vulnerabilities.

Like everyone else, you have some bad days. You experience discouragement. You suffer from anxiety. You just want to escape the crazy whirlwind. I get it! **But part of maturing, and part of preventing a destructive collapse, is learning to tolerate these discomforts and uncertainties of life.** It's learning to sit in our distress, to pause when we realize we're vulnerable, to invite God to examine our hearts and speak truth to us, and to look far enough ahead of our decisions to discern their benefit (or their danger). If you're concerned about wrecking your life and you can see present dangers, I encourage you to pause. Maybe others have sounded a warning, but you don't see the problem. It's time to pay attention to those warning signals.

PONDER THAT!

Take some time, right now, to inspect your situation.

Consider your vulnerabilities. Do you detect the presence of isolation, comparison, boredom, despair, or pride? Take an objective peek at your coping skills. Are they helpful? Or are they causing you to spiral? Take inventory of your mental state. Are you hurting so badly that you've missed the warnings about potential consequences? Do you just want an escape? Are you responding impulsively? Are you having a difficult time regulating your emotions? Are you stable enough to make life-altering decisions?

Consider your spiritual state. Are you far from God? Withdrawing from brothers and sisters in Christ? Hiding? Are you drawing comfort and wisdom from His Word? Is prayer a burden or a delight?

Consider your recent pattern of decisions (and the future-focused decisions you're pondering). Are you dabbling with disaster? Are you on the brink of a decision that will create permanent heartache? Can you in good conscience recommend others take the same path you're considering?

If you are concerned about an implosion, know that there is still time for damage control! Speak with a trusted friend. Call a pastor. Consult with a counselor. You have the freedom to self-destruct, but you also have the freedom to prevent a crisis. You have the freedom to protect your testimony and your reputation. You have the freedom to save your marriage or your ministry. If your check engine light is indicating potential danger, it may be time for a U-turn!

If you're struggling today, pre-implosion, reach out to a friend, mentor, pastor, or counselor who can help you re-route and prevent an unnecessary crisis.

If you are struggling today, post-implosion, reach out for help as you walk through the consequences. Remember the God who welcomes the prodigal and desires to rebuild the ruins. Nothing is impossible for Him!

VERSE OF HOPE

They shall build up the ancient ruins; they shall raise up the former devastations; they shall repair the ruined cities, the devastations of many generations.
—*Isaiah 61:4*

MY PRAYER FOR YOU TODAY

God, I pray for my friends who are reading this devotion today.

Give them eyes to see any vulnerability that could wreck their lives. Guide them as they safely, honestly, and thoroughly evaluate their coping skills, their mental state, their emotional state, their spiritual state, and their patterns of decisions. Give them an objective view of their lives.

Shackle the enemy and expose any attempts to deceive.

Put people in their lives who can be guardrails.

And protect them from an unnecessary implosion that would sabotage their bounce!

Father, thank You for welcoming the one who is walking through the consequences of an implosion today. Thank You for Your grace-lavished response to repentance and Your promise to rebuild the ruins. Nothing is impossible for You.

And no previous implosion prevents a new bounce!

THINK AND PRAY

What is God revealing about your vulnerabilities, your coping skills, your mental state, your emotional state, your spiritual state, and your patterns of decisions?

Are you vulnerable to an implosion right now?

If you've experienced an implosion in the past, how are you recovering? What do you need to make real progress?

Make my prayer your own.

 # UNRESOLVED SIN

Many things can jeopardize our mental health, but the one thing we most dislike to explore is . . . sin. Uncomfortable. But true.

Sadly, it's also the first thing we're likely to point out in another person who is struggling. So, let's tread this topic carefully and accurately.

Some Christians believe that every heartache has a clear cause and effect, and the cause is always our sin. But unconfessed sin isn't always the underlying problem in mental health struggles. Consider the blind man referenced in John 9. When asked to explain this man's affliction, Jesus replied, "It was not that this man sinned, or his parents, but that the works of God might be displayed in him" (v. 3). This is an example of our need to take great care to avoid making the false assumption that pain or suffering is always due to sin. This absolute is a biblically impossible conclusion.

But it *is* true that unrepentant sin always keeps us stuck and prevents recovery. That absolute is a biblically accurate conclusion.

With that said, if you are clinging to something selfish or destructive, or someone that God has been prompting you to escape, you will continue to experience a higher level of mental health symptoms until you respond. **Because sin invites unnecessary symptoms and unnecessary suffering.**

PONDER THAT!

Be honest with yourself about any unconfessed sin. If you can identify an area of sin that you need to address, consider how this unresolved issue has been impacting your thoughts, your emotional health, your behaviors, your physical wellbeing, your relationships, your finances, and your spiritual life.

If you notice emotional symptoms of guilt, stress, or anxiety, it's possible that these emotional responses are the prompting of the Holy Spirit, intended to guide you out of a situation that's separating you from God and destructive to your life. If your behaviors indicate that you are trying to hide something from God or others, then you are undoubtedly experiencing distress. But you aren't trapped. There's a way out. The painful emotions and awkward behaviors are indicating that it is time for a U-turn. Today, acknowledge your sin to God

(He knows it already), and run to the Father. Know that He desires your freedom. And He's running toward you with open arms!

If you don't identify any area of unconfessed sin, simply thank God for His forgiveness and your closeness with Him, and don't get stuck on any false guilt or condemnation.

VERSE OF HOPE

I acknowledged my sin to you, and I did not cover my iniquity; I said, "I will confess my transgressions to the Lord," and you forgave the iniquity of my sin. —*Psalm 32:5*

MY PRAYER FOR YOU TODAY

God, I pray for my friend who is reading this devotion today.

I pray You will give them the courage today to search their hearts. Reveal any area of sin that is holding them captive. That is oppressing them. That is the root of their racing thoughts and rushing emotions. God, remove any deception that prevents them from seeing truth regarding unconfessed sin. Regarding a stronghold. Regarding a trap they never intended to be caught in.

Father, remind them of Your safety. Your grace. Your radical capacity to forgive. Invite them to stop running and find peace in being still in Your presence, admitting to You what You already know. God, rescue them from the stress of covering their sin and be near as they navigate the consequences of their choices. Thank You for the blood of Jesus that covers everything that was previously hidden. Shock them with relief and hope as they discover that releasing sin is an essential element of their bounce.

And God, I pray for protection from condemnation or false guilt for those whose walk is clear. For those who are seeking You with all their heart, who are quick to confess their sin, and who are suffering right now in ways that have nothing to do with sin and are only understood in the spiritual realm. Be near and give them comfort as they continue their journey with resilience.

THINK AND PRAY

How do you discern when you are experiencing conviction of the Holy Spirit in contrast to false guilt?

Are you currently experiencing symptoms that are related to unconfessed sin?

If so, what is feeding that habit in your life? Are you ready to release it?

If not, how are you managing any false guilt (from yourself or others) that might wiggle its way into your mind?

Make my prayer your own.

 # KNOWN AND LOVED

Unless you're living under a rock, your life, like mine, is peppered by pain and sin. Maybe too much pepper. Disappointment. Mistakes. Hurt. Betrayal. Relationship struggles. Regret. Because life really is hard.

The pain that peppers our lives often causes us to draw false conclusions that we aren't worthy of love and acceptance. And emotions of shame and loneliness.

Most of us have a core fear about being fully known, with the internal dialogue, "If you really knew me, you wouldn't like me." **And at our core we also doubt being fully loved.**

So we keep our walls up and protect our vulnerability. Wrestling with doubt becomes our chronic tension this side of heaven.

Yet, we all have a core need for being thoroughly known and deeply loved. Pastor and author Tim Keller writes, "It is what we need more than anything. It liberates us from pretense, humbles us out of our self-righteousness, and fortifies us for any difficulty life can throw at us."1 Only when we experience the safety of genuine love and acceptance can we grow in relationships, feel secure in attachments, care for others radically, be courageous in decisions, and find confidence in the person God has created us to be. Being known and loved is crucial.

If you're feeling broken today, it is important to know the facts related to this dilemma. You may not experience being known and loved in your human relationships. But consider David's prayer as he reflects in awe that God knows him intimately: "O Lord, you have searched me and known me! You know when I sit down and when I rise up; you discern my thoughts from afar. You search out my path and my lying down and are acquainted with all my ways. Even before a word is on my tongue, behold, O Lord, you know it altogether" (Psalm 139:1-4).

And later in the same Psalm, David acknowledges that God had known him since before the womb, "My frame was not hidden from you, when I was being made in secret, intricately woven in the depths of the earth. Your eyes saw my unformed substance; in your book were written, every one of them, the days that were formed for me, when as yet there was none of them." (vv. 15-16)

You are known! Your Creator has *always* known you. And He knows you completely, even in your deepest and darkest places. He knows the best about you. And the worst about you.

He understands everything about you. And He loves you still.

And though that truth could leave you feeling naked and ashamed, God has also affirmed His radical and unconditional love for you: "But God shows his love for us in that while we were still sinners, Christ died for us" (Romans 5:8). In the midst of God's knowledge of your sin, He sacrificed His Son. **You *are* loved!**

PONDER THAT!

The truth of God's knowing, loving, and choosing us is hard to comprehend and even harder to accept, because our human limitation prevents us from ever fully knowing another person. And our sinful flesh limits our thorough and perfect love for anyone. But freedom is found in our acceptance of this truth.

You are wholly and unreservedly known, right now. And you are radically and completely loved, right now. Today, meditate on those facts. Sit with the reality that God *knows* you fully. Stay there. Breathe in that truth. Sit with the reality that God *loves* you fully. Stay there. Breathe in that truth.

Agree with God about your security in Him, give up the performance rat race to prove yourself, and relinquish your struggle to be good enough to be acceptable. Today, let your head be lifted up . . . and let your heart take courage.

VERSES OF HOPE

O Lord, you have searched me and known me! You know when I sit down and when I rise up; you discern my thoughts from afar. You search out my path and my lying down and are acquainted with all my ways. Even before a word is on my tongue, behold, O Lord, you know it altogether. —*Psalm 139:1-4*

MY PRAYER FOR YOU TODAY

God, I pray for my friends who are reading this devotion today.

They yearn to be fully known and fully loved.

But at the core, they also fear being fully known. And they doubt being fully loved.

God, I pray that You will break through their fears and doubts.
Overwhelm them with Your love and safety.
Give them assurance.

Ground them and calm them as they rest in knowing that
You know more about them than they could ever know about
themselves. Their pains and their victories. Their strengths and
their weaknesses. Their sins and their strengths.

And give them assurance that Your love is a radical love. Allow
them to experience that, right now. Please, Father, captivate
them with Your unconditional love!

I pray they will develop a secure attachment with You that
provides the strong foundation for their bounce and flows into
the meaningful relationships in their lives!

THINK AND PRAY

When you imagine being fully known, what negative thoughts come to the
surface?

How do you sometimes resist God's love?

DAY 23

You are wholly and unreservedly known. And you are radically and completely loved.

How would you like to respond to this truth about you, right now?

Make my prayer your own.

 # SILENCING SHAME

Past decisions that you regret. Memories that make you cringe. Seasons of humiliation. It's so easy to get stuck on a shame-inducing memory lane. We easily attach ourselves to the regretful decisions of our past. We give tremendous power to our former mistakes, sins, and the negative experiences of our history.

We fall to our knees in repentance for our sin, but too often we still give our regrets self-defining authority, opening the door to years of self-induced punishment and shame. **The memory lane of regret invites shame to have a voice, keeps us stuck, influences our decisions, impacts our relationships, and compromises our mental health.**

Let's look to the Scriptures for some guidance about silencing our shame. David, after committing adultery and murdering the spouse of his mistress, was later referred to by God as "a man after my heart" (Acts 13:22). In the cleansing of God's forgiveness, *his shame was silenced.*

Paul, after persecuting Christians, was inspired by the Spirit to write much of the New Testament. *Shame was silenced!*

These men serve as evidence that, for the repentant heart, there is no partial forgiveness. **God is radical in His desire to rescue us from our sin and silence our shame.** Let's rejoice with gratitude that God wants us to bounce forward, beyond the memory and defining power of "former things" (Isaiah 43:18).

PONDER THAT!

Today, treasure the truth that God accepts your request for forgiveness because He already paid the price for it when Christ took your place on the cross. Jesus took our sins so we could receive His love, forgiveness, and acceptance. And He responds gladly to your repentance. So thorough is God's forgiveness that when He looks at you, He sees you "holy and blameless," thanks to Jesus (Ephesians 1:3-4). Write a letter to yourself today, as if written by God directly to you, releasing you from your shame. Replace it with the truth of God's amazing grace. Refuse to continue rehearsing your shame, and begin the journey of embracing God's truth about you.

VERSES OF HOPE

Remember not the former things,
nor consider the things of old.
Behold, I am doing a new thing;
now it springs forth, do you not perceive it?
I will make a way in the wilderness
and rivers in the desert.
—*Isaiah 43:18-19*

MY PRAYER FOR YOU TODAY

God, I pray for my friends who are reading this devotion today.

They know the pain of regret. The sting of shame. It's impossible to forget.

God, fill them with the reassurance that their repentance is enough. Thank You, God, for rescuing them from their past sin through Christ's sacrifice.

Thank You for silencing their shame, lifting their face, and giving them permission to "remember not the former things."

And when the whispers of shame come back to knock on their door, remind them not to answer. Not to listen. Not to believe. For there is no partial forgiveness with You, Father. Your gift of forgiveness is thorough and sufficient.

Shame has no seat at their table.

God, give them confidence in Your forgiveness so that they will refuse to listen to the dark whispers. Thank You for washing away their shame, making a way in their wilderness, creating a river in their desert, and paving the road to a better future!

THINK AND PRAY

What has the voice of shame spoken about you?

What is God's truth about His amazing grace toward you? How would you describe His love and forgiveness?

How are you feeling about embracing God's truth about you?

We don't have selective amnesia, so what does it mean to "remember not the former things"?

Make my prayer your own.

 RUN TOWARD GRACE

You have regrets. I know. We all do. Some days you may be haunted by those regrets. Perhaps today is one of those days. If so, your tears may be your closest companion.

Regret is tough because there is no one else to blame. And the consequences were once preventable. **You may find it hard to live with your regret. Hard to hide your regret. Hard to fix the consequences.** More than anything, you may feel trapped by your regret.

We've all been there. We all have a sinful nature. We've all made choices we wish we could rewind and correct. But I'm here to remind you of One who loved you so much that **He submitted to His crucifixion so He could bear your burden, cover your sinful choices, redeem your messes, and cast away your regrets. Because He really loves you.**

Today may be the first time that anyone has encouraged you to consider Jesus. That means today may represent the most important day of your life. Or maybe you've already considered Jesus and have trusted Him before. This is the day you are *reminded* of His incredibly radical love for you . . . and how His love speaks to your regrets. Consider this: When Jesus came forward to be arrested before His crucifixion, He was preparing to take our place and bear the judgment we deserve. On the cross, He bore the sins of the liar, the thief, the abuser, the adulterer, the addict, the murderer. He was providing a covering for the sinful choices that you regret today. *He took it all on.*

Jesus wore your sin like a garment on that cross so that He could give you the greatest gift you've never deserved.

Which means that you don't have to keep walking in shame.

You don't have to keep walking in darkness.

You don't have to keep walking in oppression.

You don't have to keep living without hope.

Your hope became personalized when Jesus gave himself up and took the penalty for your sin. And you have the opportunity to gain hope today by accepting the gift that you could never earn.

We learn in the Scriptures about two of Jesus' disciples who took radically different approaches to their regrets. Both had walked with Jesus. Both had shared meals with Him and had meaningful conversations with Him. Both had misunderstood Him and had betrayed Him. Both were overwhelmed with sorrow about their sin and verbalized their regret. But there was one significant difference between them: **Judas ran *from* Jesus. But Peter ran *toward* Jesus.**

Judas, filled with regret over his sin, tried to fix his mess and make things right on his own. When he couldn't, he committed suicide. It didn't have to be that way. Peter, grieved regarding his sin, *knew that he couldn't make it right on his own,* so he sought forgiveness and release from his shame. Jesus restored him, and Peter went on to live a life of purpose. In fact, not only did Peter have hope, but he became a giver of hope!

PONDER THAT!

You don't have to continue to be haunted by regrets over past sins. Immerse yourself in revisiting the crucifixion. Right now, in this very moment, visualize your sin and your regrets like a garment on your Savior. He died to cover that sin and release those regrets. Today, allow yourself to stop running from your regrets in shame, and instead, run toward His grace, with repentance. You don't have to be trapped anymore! Jesus died to save you and is lovingly waiting for you to remember that He has already paid the price to forgive you. It's done. It's over. It's finished. If you've already trusted Jesus, let your soul be *reminded* today of His incredibly radical love for you. Pay attention to what His love speaks to your regrets as you consider His crucifixion.

VERSE OF HOPE

"Lord, you know everything. You know that I love you." —*John 21:17*

MY PRAYER FOR YOU TODAY

God, I pray for my friends who are reading this devotion today.

I know they have regrets because we all do.

If shame is hindering their resilience, reveal it right now and speak truth to their regrets.

I pray You would pursue those who haven't trusted You, and who are stuck in their shame, struggling to find rescue. God, give them the courage to invite Your rescue, right now.

Father, remind Your children that their regrets are covered. If they are running away, guide them to turn around. To run toward You, not away from You. Thank You for always welcoming Your children with open arms!

Welcome them as they run to You for cover.

THINK AND PRAY

What are the regrets that came to your mind during today's devotion?

Which direction have you been running? From Jesus or toward Jesus?

What would it mean for you to run to Jesus?

Make my prayer your own.

Paul often spoke of running a race and the endurance required for such a physical challenge. Many can run a sprint but fewer can run a marathon because it requires such perseverance. That kind of long-suffering is as much mental as it is physical.

If you are in a hard season, you already know that the race out of depression, anxiety, loneliness, or discouragement and toward emotional security is more like a marathon than a sprint. Unfortunately, much like we are in a long and grueling race, our tendency is to quit. In our discouragement, we may not see how things can get better, so we figuratively throw up our hands.

We give up. And far too often, we give up prematurely. Do you feel like quitting today? Are you weary? Are you thirsty for an ending, and you don't feel like it is coming soon enough? Do you feel like you're slipping away and just can't hold on?

I don't know what you have considered quitting. Maybe it's your marriage. Maybe it's your job. Maybe it's a friendship. Maybe it's parenting. Maybe it's ministry. Maybe it's God. Maybe it is life itself.

Your enemy would love nothing more than for you to give up on living, hopeless that things could get better. But then your race would end before the finish line. It's a premature end that confuses and devastates those who are watching. And it doesn't have to be.

No matter your area of weariness, there is always a way out of the trap. And it may not require quitting. Maybe it just requires a pause. A breather. A friend to help you regroup so that you can get back into the race.

Some situations and people really do have to be released. You must let them go. But before you decide to give up anything (including yourself), find a wise and godly friend who can help you think through your decisions. Someone who can help you see your blind spots. Who can help you identify your all-or-nothing thinking. Who can help you problem-solve and seek solutions. We all need someone in the ditch with us, for "Where there is no guidance, a people falls, but in an abundance of counselors there is safety" (Proverbs 11:14). David had Jonathan. Naomi had Ruth. John Mark had Barnabas. Esther had Mordecai. Scripture is full of inspiring heroes who depended on other people to help them finish their race. There's no shame in needing help.

If you're on the verge of giving up, ask God to lead you to the right person to be in the ditch with you. Someone who is loyal. Someone who can lift your arms and your soul when you are weary, and pick you up when you fall. Someone who will love you, and not be intimidated by your resistance. Someone who can flood you with a beautiful balance of truth and grace. *Someone who won't let you quit your race. And who won't guilt you into staying in a race you should release.*

Someone who points you to Jesus! Someone who is sometimes running ahead of you. Sometimes running behind you. And always running beside you, with eyes on the eternal finish line.

You have a race to finish, my friend! It's YOUR race! Finish well.

PONDER THAT!

Yes, you have a race to finish. Imagine God fueling you with the strength to persevere, the wisdom to understand, and the passion and enthusiasm to finish your fight and run your race. Never give up! Keep the faith! Finish well!

If you are weary and considering giving up on a task or a relationship prematurely, pray about who you need beside you. Today, send a text or make a phone call to that person. Tell them about today's devotion and the weariness you feel.

If you are thinking about giving up on your life, call a mentor, pastor, counselor, or physician—right now! You can also contact the national hotline by dialing 988 or go to the nearest Emergency Room. Ending your life is a forever decision, and you need someone to help you think through all the angles of a big decision like that. Pause any plans to end your life and talk through this decision with someone you can trust.

VERSE OF HOPE

I have fought the good fight, I have finished the race, I have kept the faith. *—2 Timothy 4:7*

MY PRAYER FOR YOU TODAY

God, I pray for my friends who are reading this devotion today.

Quitting is such a temptation when we're running a race and we don't see the end. When we're weary and discouraged.

Lord, give my friends discernment about when they are to release. And when they are to fight and persevere. Give them the strength, energy, motivation, and drive to continue moving forward. Give them the faith to continue toward the unseen finish line.

Give them the people they need.

Their Barnabas. Their Ruth. Their Jonathan. Their Mordecai.

Father, I know that the race is messy because the process to resilience is messy.

They've been thrown to the ground, and their bounce forward is right out of a mudhole. It's emotionally, physically, mentally, spiritually, and relationally messy.

Help my friends to bounce! To tolerate the messiness. To continue to fight the good fight, finish the race, and keep the faith!

THINK AND PRAY

When have you felt like giving up? What was going on that made you feel so hopeless?

Consider times in your past when you gave up prematurely. What did those experiences teach you?

How have mentors given you perspective, inspiration, or wisdom in previous difficulties?

How have friends motivated you to keep going when you wanted to quit?

Make my prayer your own.

DO YOU WANT TO BE HEALED?

You are accustomed to feeling anxious or panicked. Thoughts of inadequacy are frequent and familiar. Discouragement wears like a blanket. Tears are never far away.

But I have an honest question. No one is looking. No one waiting for your reply. No timer hurrying your answer. Go ahead, search your heart deeply. Sit here for a while with this question. **Do you want to be healed? Really?**

Allow yourself to be immersed in that question for just a moment more. *Do you want to be healed?* Notice any hint of resistance. Of hesitation. Of discomfort. Of fear. Note any tension in your body brought about by contemplating that question.

Only a physician who understands the fear of becoming well would even know to ask such a brazen question. The perfect physician, Jesus, asked this question to the invalid of thirty-eight years, referenced in John 5:6. **If Jesus asked the question, perhaps we *also* should ask the question. Because it's a fair inquiry.**

The truth is that *our pain can become our identity*, so strongly enmeshed with our sense of self that it prevents healing. Sometimes we remain stuck in our physical and emotional suffering simply because our painful state becomes oddly comfortable. Our pain becomes familiar. Our depression becomes predictable. Anxiety becomes routine. Expectations remain low in a chronic state of oppression. And breaking through the stronghold into genuine hope and productive action can be quite daunting.

Sometimes we're afraid to be well. So we stay stuck. And forfeit our opportunity to bounce.

PONDER THAT!

Consider how your suffering has attached to your identity. While it's normal to have anxiety regarding an unknown future, empowered fear can keep you stuck. What are your specific concerns related to becoming healthy and active? How do those concerns stunt your growth and create a ceiling that obstructs your bounce forward? *Do you want to be healed?*

VERSES OF HOPE

One man was there who had been an invalid for thirty-eight years. When Jesus saw him lying there and knew that he had already been there a long time, he said to him, "Do you want to be healed?" —*John 5:5-6*

MY PRAYER FOR YOU TODAY

God, I pray for my friends who are reading this devotion today.

I know that change is scary. Even the magnificent and wonderful changes of healing and hope can be daunting. Because anything unknown, even hope, causes anxiety.

God, I pray that You would reveal any hint of hesitation that could sabotage healing. In this moment, right now, I pray that You would speak reassuring truth to any fears that may block a bounce.

Thank you, Jesus, for modeling this essential question. It's a fair question, and I pray that the hearts of my friends would be soft to evaluate carefully and provide an honest answer.

Today, speak to every sensation of reluctance. Increase our tolerance for the discomforts of healing and change. And rescue my friends from the sabotage of fear, fully releasing them so they settle for nothing less than the resilience You have destined for them!

THINK AND PRAY

Today, how do you honestly answer the question, "Do you want to be healed?"

Name any hindrance, hesitation, or reluctance.

What would you speak to another friend who shared those hesitations?

Make my prayer your own.

DAY 28 TAKE EVERY THOUGHT CAPTIVE

A significant aspect of our battle for mental health is a battle of the mind. God knew it would be this way, and He has given us sufficient instruction and help for our role in training our brains to assertively manage our thoughts. **You and I are instructed to "take every thought captive."**

Captive—that's a strong word. It's a word that illustrates the passivity created by our helpless, hopeless, worthless internal dialogue. We're prisoners of our shame. So often, we're casual with our thoughts. Utterly unaware of their power.

But the word can be used to describe a much better purpose. We're to *capture* a toxic defeating thought rather than passively allowing it to mature and grow. We're instructed to be mindful of our thinking, and to *incarcerate* a destructive, false narrative about ourselves, about God, about another person, about our past, about our current situation, or about our future.

This active obedience of capturing our destructive thoughts is very important. Why? **Because with every thought, there is a chemical release,** which means that our failure to take thoughts captive has a negative consequence to the health of our brains.

We physically nurture our brains when we capture destructive thoughts and fuel healthy thoughts based on God's truth.

The process of taking thoughts captive changes the brain! And when you change your brain, you change everything.

Today and in the next two devotions, we'll focus on replacing false beliefs with God's truth. Why three devotions on one topic? Because it's so important!

PONDER THAT!

Today, embrace the reality that your thoughts change your brain, for good or bad. Make it a point today to take any destructive thought captive. Find a tool that assists you in arresting your thoughts. Here are a few examples: Write out your destructive thought and then burn or shred the paper. Or imagine that thought on a chalkboard in your mind, and then take your mental eraser and wipe it clean. Or imagine having an indestructible "negative thought prison" on a shelf in your mind where you can effectively incarcerate these thoughts. Consider how you are nurturing your brain when you take your thoughts captive. And imagine the release of healthy chemicals into your mind with every shift in your thinking.

VERSE OF HOPE

We destroy arguments and every lofty opinion raised against the knowledge of God, and take every thought captive to obey Christ. —*2 Corinthians 10:5*

MY PRAYER FOR YOU TODAY

God, I pray for my friends who are reading this devotion today.

Give them eyes to see Your design of their brain and the beautiful privilege You have given them to manage their thoughts. Give them specific awareness of destructive thoughts. Design for them an indestructible prison in their minds where they can incarcerate their damaging thoughts. Guide them with truth as You transform their thinking and change their brains. Bring stability to their emotions as they submit their thoughts to You, and guide them with wisdom in their responses to other people and circumstances.

Thank You for the beautiful design of the brain. Heal their minds as they submit their thoughts in obedience to You.

THINK AND PRAY

How would a "negative thought prison" work for you?

What tool have you discovered that helps you to capture your destructive thoughts?

What are two or three passages of Scripture that encourage you deeply? How would replacing destructive thoughts with these truths make a difference in your outlook . . . and your brain?

Identifying negative patterns of thought, imprisoning them, and replacing them with encouraging truth is a skill everyone can master. What do you think the process of mastery will look like in your life?

Make my prayer your own.

THINK ON THESE THINGS

It's so easy to let a negative, destructive thought take over. **Unfortunately, something so easy to overlook will subtly, but certainly, make a mess.**

"I'm not good enough."

"Things will never get better."

"I've missed my opportunity for the life I wanted."

"I'm stupid."

"I hate this job."

"I'm a horrible parent."

"If they really knew me, they wouldn't like me."

Sound familiar? If you have destructive thoughts, you have a set of frequent, familiar, and toxic narratives on a replay loop in your mind. Until now, you may not have even realized you had those thoughts. Thoughts that are subtly negative. Others that are aggressively negative. **You may feel like you're married to these thoughts . . . like they are a part of who you are and you don't know how to live life without them.**

They seem very, very familiar. Maybe even comfortable in a strange way. And maybe you have concluded that these thoughts are helpful to you. The problem? **Those destructive thoughts eventually become automatic thoughts, ruling your emotions, and dictating your responses to life.**

Read that again. Let it sink in. Those automatic negative thoughts are ruling your emotions and dictating your responses to life. Because destructive thoughts make a mess.

It's why I call our negative internal narrative "The Most Important Conversation No One Ever Heard." Destructive thoughts create hidden pathways that become the most influential aspect of our lives, often ruling our emotions and dictating our behaviors.

But God has provided the instruction (and the content) for replacement thoughts. If we want mental wellness, we must identify the negative narrative. Then we need to starve the beast and replace the familiar, destructive thoughts that have held us captive for too, too long.

Thoughts matter!

PONDER THAT!

Today, you will catch yourself in a negative thought. When God makes you aware of this thought, pivot from the destructive thought to one that is "true . . . honorable . . . just . . . pure . . . lovely . . . commendable . . . and worthy of praise" (Philippians 4:8). If your destructive thoughts are making a mess of your emotions and your responses to people and situations, take the risk of sharing this struggle with a trusted friend and ask them to hold you accountable in your thought life.

VERSE OF HOPE

Finally, brothers, whatever is true, whatever is honorable, whatever is just, whatever is pure, whatever is lovely, whatever is commendable, if there is any excellence, if there is anything worthy of praise, think about these things. —*Philippians 4:8*

MY PRAYER FOR YOU TODAY

God, I pray for my friends who are reading this devotion today.

I trust that You will make them aware of any pattern of negative thinking today. God, give them the courage to be honest about their internal dialogue, and give them insights regarding the negative impact this silent struggle is having on their emotions and responses. I pray You will give them the words of truth that speak back to the lies. Give them the wisdom to replace these destructive patterns, one thought at a time.

Help them submit their thoughts to You. And give them the mind of Christ, with thoughts that are true . . . honorable . . . just . . . pure . . . lovely . . . commendable . . . and worthy of praise.

Bring along someone who can support them as they work to identify and transform their thoughts.

Father, thank You for the blessing of the mind and for its power in the journey of resilience.

THINK AND PRAY

Today, you identified some of your negative thoughts. Thoughts that have been present for a long time. Write down the most familiar, repetitive toxic thoughts that are influencing your emotions and responses to life.

Now, for every destructive thought you identified, write out an adjusted statement that is true . . . honorable . . . just . . . pure . . . lovely . . . commendable . . . and worthy of praise.

What, or who, will help you to *"think about these things"*?

Make my prayer your own.

DAY 30 THE GIFT OF NEUROPLASTICITY

Neuroplasticity: this may just be the most important and hopeful word you've read all week! Let's simplify this large and imposing word: *neuroplasticity* just means that our brains can change. Our brains are indeed adaptable and can be rewired. In practical terms, this means that if you've had a traumatic brain injury or a stroke, there is hope for some recovery. It also means great hope for those who experience psychological distress.

Imagine this: By changing the toxic thought patterns of the mind, we can change the brain . . . which then changes the emotions . . . which then changes our responses. As we've seen, **changing the brain changes everything!**

How? Romans 12:2 reveals our answer: "Do not be conformed to this world, but be transformed by the renewal of your mind, that by testing you may discern what is the will of God, what is good and acceptable and perfect." If the brain is malleable, then toxic beliefs and thoughts about ourselves, our past, our current circumstances, and our future can destructively mold the brain, creating and exacerbating struggles like anxiety and depression. But imagine the impact of a radically different thought process, one that is founded on truth and doesn't "conform to this world."

That is a transformational replacement that results in transformed emotions and behaviors, which cascade into every area of our lives!

God created our brains to respond beautifully when we obey His commands regarding our thoughts. He rewards this obedience with healing and health. **Replacing toxic beliefs with God's truths releases chemicals that literally change the brain and provide the ability to overcome many psychological struggles.**

PONDER THAT!

Neuroplasticity: it's a beautiful gift for mental health, granted by an amazing Creator! Today, notice your thoughts and imagine your brain becoming healthier as your toxic thoughts are conquered and replaced. Focus on submitting your thoughts to God, rejecting destructive beliefs, and meditating on truth about yourself, your situation, and your God.

VERSE OF HOPE

Do not be conformed to this world, but be transformed by the renewal of your mind, that by testing you may discern what is the will of God, what is good and acceptable and perfect. —*Romans 12:2*

MY PRAYER FOR YOU TODAY

God, I pray for my friends who are reading this devotion today.

Encourage them as they ponder Your great
gift of neuroplasticity.

Today, alert them to any destructive thoughts that hijack their emotional health and influence their behaviors. Guide them as they cooperate with You, submitting those destructive thoughts to You, allowing You to heal their minds as they
navigate life's challenges.

Father, I ask that You renew their minds with thoughts that are
pleasing to You.

Thank You for being a perfect, masterful Creator.

Thank You for designing a brain that can adapt beautifully when thoughts are managed Your way!

I pray You will finish what You've started and
help them bounce forward.

THINK AND PRAY

Write down the negative thoughts that are causing you to feel discouraged today.

How are those thoughts impacting your emotions and your behaviors?

Cross out the negative thoughts written above, and then write out a more compassionate and truthful thought for each negative thought that you listed. What do you notice about how this replacement shifts your emotional response?

Make my prayer your own.

I live in North Carolina where we are blessed to have four distinct seasons. I love the change of seasons. The outside temperature changes. Foliage changes. Clothing changes. I especially love spring, with the bursting of fresh leaves and bright blooms that beautifully contrast the dead of winter. The transition to spring-like weather is certainly a welcomed one. But let's be honest—not all transitions are welcome.

Today, you may be experiencing an overwhelmingly tough change, and you just don't know how you'll adapt. **The truth is, you might not even** want **to adapt**. You may feel paralyzed by fear, with thoughts of despair. You may just want to stay in bed because facing the day seems to be too much.

I must confess that I don't have much tolerance for cold weather, but I've found a great coping skill. Layers! My husband laughs when he sees my layers, but I remind him that my clothing choices are always better than my whining. He agrees and encourages the use of my special trick for cold weather.

If you're experiencing an unwelcome change, you may feel the urge to resist it. You may have negative thoughts. You'll probably tend to whine and complain (because you're human and you're tempted to verbalize the destructive thoughts that are on repeat in your mind).

Remember, resisting an ordained change in your life will keep you stuck and will dishonor God. And if we're honest, we know that frequent whining about change emotionally drains those we love.

So, whatever your change, find some "layers"—some ways of coping that allow you to embrace the adjustment. Challenge your destructive thoughts about your transition and replace them with thoughts of hope.

PONDER THAT!

Today, consider how you might maneuver through a challenging transition with "layers" of creative, effective coping skills. Take some time to brainstorm your options. Ask a friend, mentor, pastor, or counselor to help you build a toolbox of coping skills. Develop specific strategies and thank God that, though He sometimes orchestrates change in our lives, He himself never changes.

VERSE OF HOPE

For I the Lord do not change. —*Malachi 3:6*

MY PRAYER FOR YOU TODAY

God, I pray for my friends who are reading this devotion today.

Remind them that You never change.

No matter the chaos and uncertainty they face, You are the same. You are always faithful.

Safe. Ever-present.

Father, guide them as they brainstorm coping skills that would be helpful for this challenging season. Give them wisdom as they discern the "layers" that are helpful for them and honoring to You. Give them strength and encouragement to adapt to the necessary changes ahead.

Thank You for Your steadfast love during tough seasons of change.

Your constant presence faithfully facilitates their bounce.

THINK AND PRAY

List the changes you are experiencing. Which of them inspire creativity and hope, and which ones are daunting?

If this was someone else's list, how might this season of change impact them?

What specific strategies would you advise for a person in a similar situation?

God never changes. How does that fact impact your emotional response today?

Make my prayer your own.

DAY 32 GROUNDING

Our bodies are truly remarkable. They serve as evidence that we have more tools to manage our mental health than we might realize. Consider our senses. God has gifted us with the ability . . .

To see.

To smell.

To taste.

To hear.

To touch.

Our senses allow us to interact with the world around us and alert us to danger.

And our senses bring us great joy! Can you imagine life without your physical senses? Many people live without vision or hearing, but can you imagine a life completely void of all five of the senses? Nothing to see. Nothing to smell. Nothing to taste. Nothing to hear. Nothing to touch. It's unfathomable because our senses are remarkable gifts that most of us have never been without.

What an extravagant gift! God could have created us more simply. But He didn't. **Our senses allow us to experience an explosion of sensations that add richness to life and are a reason to worship.**

Even more, these senses that add color and satisfaction to life are also great tools for grounding mental health symptoms! Petting a dog or cat can provide comfort. Listening to a bird sing changes our focus from anxious thoughts to delight. Seeing a beautiful scene reminds us that God is present and creative.

Engaging the senses calms anxiety and PTSD and can also be grounding for dissociation and psychosis. Our Creator gave us an amazing tool, and we have the privilege of maximizing that gift.

PONDER THAT!

Today, enjoy the fresh air, take in the pleasant aromas, notice the variety of tastes in a wonderful dish, and feel the warmth of the sunshine on your face and the grass below your feet. Notice the brilliant colors you see and the sounds of the birds chirping. Allow God to meet you through awareness of your senses, and thank Him for it all. Linger and worship Him for His generous gift! Notice how God calms your symptoms as you engage your senses.

VERSES OF HOPE

That which was from the beginning, which we have heard, which we have seen with our eyes, which we looked upon and have touched with our hands, concerning the word of life—the life was made manifest, and we have seen it, and testify to it and proclaim to you the eternal life, which was with the Father and was made manifest to us—that which we have seen and heard we proclaim also to you, so that you too may have fellowship with us; and indeed our fellowship is with the Father and with his Son Jesus Christ. And we are writing these things so that our joy may be complete. —*1 John 1:1-4*

MY PRAYER FOR YOU TODAY

God, I pray for my friends who are reading this devotion today.

Remind them of Your radical love for them, that You would create something so unique and luxurious as the ability to see. To smell. To taste. To Touch. To hear.

You didn't have to be so extravagant. But You were.

I pray that You would bless them with calmness as they engage their senses. Remind them that You are near as they look at their surroundings right now, as they smell the aromas right now, as they notice the cool air or the warm breeze on their skin right now, as they taste and know that You are good, and as they hear the sounds that remind them that they are in this present moment. Not the past. Not the future.

Just here in this moment. Now.

I pray that they would be at peace in Your presence.

THINK AND PRAY

What do you see, smell, hear, taste, and touch, right now?

What did you notice about how this brief observation of your senses calmed you and grounded you?

What difference will it make to develop a habit of being more aware of your senses?

What are some practical steps you can take to be more aware of them every day, and in fact, several times a day?

Make my prayer your own.

Isn't it amazing that God created us with the capacity to feel emotions?

Much like our senses, our emotions can add great stimulation and satisfaction to our lives. Our emotional capacity is a great blessing! A luxurious gift!

Just think of a handful of the emotions that we're capable of experiencing: Joy. Embarrassment. Sadness. Ecstasy. Anger. Shame. Pride. Shock. Anticipation. Regret. Disgust. And many, many more. Our capacity for emotions is far, far more extensive and complex than this list. We can feel blends of different emotions, and we can sometimes feel conflicting emotions at the same time. Some emotions we enjoy deeply because they bring us great pleasure. But we do our best to avoid others. They are painful. Even torturous. Strong emotions can even be felt in our body. A lump in the throat. A heavy heart. An increased pulse. Butterflies in the stomach. What an incredible, intangible, invisible, and intriguing gift!

But, like any other gift or blessing, our emotions require management and regulation, as they all too easily invite unnecessary suffering. And our emotions are terrible decision-makers!

Consider fear. Fear is an incredibly helpful and necessary emotion that alerts us to danger and prompts us to be vigilant and seek safety. But excessive fear can cause us to panic and lead us to withdraw from situations where we need to stay engaged. Fear is not a bad emotion—it's one of God's gifts—but it must be managed.

Consider happiness. A fleeting emotion of intense satisfaction. We all love to feel happy, and we're thankful when we have experiences or seasons of happiness. But sometimes we create suffering because we'll do almost anything to *achieve* happiness. And we'll do even more to *keep* feeling happy! Our craving for happiness can even compromise our convictions and tempt us to do things we wouldn't typically do because we want to experience the adrenaline rush. Happiness is not bad—it's another of God's gifts—but it must be managed.

Our emotions are neither good nor bad. Not just something to achieve or something to avoid, but tools we've been given and blessings to be managed.

I like to think of emotions like the check engine light on a car. Our emotions give us data. They can indicate potential complications or even the need to figuratively pause, pull over, and check things out. But just like a check engine light can't drive a car, our emotions are awful drivers of our decisions and must be supervised.

Our emotions can deceive us, so let's be aware of their benefits and the snares that can so easily distract or overwhelm us.

PONDER THAT!

Pray with *thankfulness* regarding the blessing of your emotions. And then pray for *discernment* so your emotions will be your "check engine light" to guard against awarding your emotions undue power. Take note of the power of your various emotions today, as well as your ability to regulate them.

VERSE OF HOPE

The heart is deceitful above all things,
and desperately sick;
who can understand it?
—*Jeremiah 17:9*

MY PRAYER FOR YOU TODAY

God, I pray for my friends who are reading this devotion today.

Remind them of the gift of the emotions You created. And the purpose of those emotions. Fill them with Your Holy Spirit, who gives discernment and power to manage and regulate challenging emotions. Reveal to them any areas in which emotions are awarded too much power. Guide them as they discern the data that their emotions reveal and convict them to yield to You instead being ruled by their strong emotions.

Protect them from being deceived by their emotional responses, which seem so right but can be so wrong.

Bless them with an overflow of the emotions of joy, encouragement, and contentment.

God, thank You for using the data their emotions provide to encourage their growth.

THINK AND PRAY

What are the emotions you regularly try to activate?

What emotions do you avoid?

How are you growing in managing your emotions? What additional growth is needed?

Make my prayer your own.

Most of us recognize the acronym, LOL. The reason for its popularity? Because life is tough, and everyone truly does appreciate a good reason to laugh. **We'd rather laugh than cry.** But laughter is so much more than just an alternative to crying.

Laughter is an amazing gift of God and a crucial ingredient for our physical, emotional, and relational health. Laughter produces a release of hormones and neurotransmitters (endorphins, dopamine, serotonin, oxytocin, etc.). These powerhouse neurochemicals are microscopic blessings from God with incalculable healing impact.

Think about the last time you enjoyed a belly laugh. Do you remember how great the experience of laughter made you feel?

Laughter is good for our emotional well-being: it reduces symptoms of depression and anxiety and improves overall mood. A deep belly laugh even brings a temporary sense of euphoria, piercing the darkness of despair.

Laughter is also good for the physical body: it lowers blood pressure, decreases stress hormones, improves the immune system, decreases pain, and helps prevent heart disease. Sounds like a good laugh is a great workout!

Laughter is even good for relationships: it reduces conflicts and strengthens bonds of friendship. We are drawn to the relationships that create laughter. Why? Because the bonding hormone, oxytocin, is released when we laugh. This hormone, also released during breastfeeding and during an orgasm, is God's design for healthy attachment.

God thought of everything when He made us, didn't He? **As if our senses and emotions weren't extravagant enough, He even gave us the ingenious capability to laugh so hard that it makes a difference in virtually every aspect of our lives. Only God could give us medicine in such a creative, powerful, and enjoyable capsule!**

PONDER THAT!

You may have experienced feelings of guilt for enjoying a moment of laughter during your difficult season. Don't allow the enemy to use false guilt to rob you of God's medicine! *If you're going through a difficult time, it's okay to laugh.*

I recommend it! Laughter is a gift of God and a salve to the soul! Today, take the prescription of laughter. Do something silly with a friend. Spend time with a group of toddlers. Take a trip to the dog park. Watch a wholesome comedy. Laughter is an essential ingredient for your bounce forward. An enjoyable gift of God designed to lift you from the muck and mire. *Embrace the opportunity to laugh today.*

VERSE OF HOPE

A joyful heart is good medicine,
but a crushed spirit dries up the bones.
—*Proverbs 17:22*

MY PRAYER FOR YOU TODAY

God, I pray for my friends who are reading this devotion today.

Thank You for bringing laughter into their season of pain.

Remind them of their permission to smile. To laugh.
To experience Joy.

I pray You use the gift of laughter to bring healing to their body.
Hope to their heart. And bonding to their relationships.

Father, surround them with triggers for belly laughs today, and
the allowance to embrace the medicine
that is a salve to their soul.

We know laughter has its place and purpose. Because You
created it, and it's good in all seasons.

Thank You for this unique and creative gift, which powerfully
propels a bounce forward.

THINK AND PRAY

How has the enemy used false guilt about laughter to keep you stuck in your pain and gloom?

When was your last deep laugh? How did you feel during and after it?

What can you do today to experience lightness, joy, and laughter?

What are some ways laughter helps you emotionally?

Physically?

Relationally?

Make my prayer your own.

You may feel like you've lost your song. **You may feel suffocated by anxiety, stress, and discouragement.** You feel like you've lost your spark, your creativity, your passion, your words. You've lost your joy.

David felt the same emotions. Paul and Silas probably also had those same emotions. They experienced all kinds of physical and emotional obstacles. **But they had a secret sauce to dispel despair that was revealed in the Old and New Testaments. They sang.**

How amazing that when God created us, He gave our bodies the beautiful capacity for things like our senses, our emotions, laughter, and the ability to make music with our voices. And each of these gifts was created for our enjoyment and His glory.

The Psalms include many of David's songs of praise during tremendous trials. And in Acts, Luke tells us that Paul and Silas sang praises so loudly in the lowest cell in a prison that others heard them (16:25). Singing is *physical*, an aerobic activity of sorts. It's also a *mental* action, an outpouring of our meditation. Singing is a *spiritual* act, an act of worship, a recognition of God's power and presence.

Singing is a whole person activity that has a powerful impact in reducing symptoms of anxiety and depression.

You may not feel like singing today, but choosing to sing anyway will engage you physically, mentally, emotionally, and spiritually, and may very well shift the trajectory of your day. Don't wait for circumstances to improve before you start singing.

PONDER THAT!

Right now is the perfect time to sing an old hymn, or turn on your favorite worship song and sing. If music has had a significant role in your life and you play an instrument, go to it now and allow yourself to be immersed in a song of praise. Notice the involvement of your entire mind and body in this amazing tool. Thank God for the gift of song, and allow the melody of your voice to not only bring Him glory, but also to refresh your joy. It's just you and God in this moment, so go ahead and lift your hands in praise, or kneel in prayer . . . and sing. Prior to this hard season, you may have been thoroughly immersed in singing and perhaps wrote your own lyrics. There is no better time to write than during a hard season. So, go ahead. This is your invitation today to get back to the tools God uniquely gifted for you.

Additionally, whether singing is a part of your history or not, consider a challenge of keeping worship music playing in the background for the next thirty days. Allow it to trigger opportunities to sing. Take note of the difference it makes in your bounce.

VERSE OF HOPE

I will sing to the Lord as long as I live;
I will sing praise to my God while I have being.
—*Psalm 104:33*

MY PRAYER FOR YOU TODAY

God, I pray for my friends who are reading this devotion today.

I know that some of them have lost their song. Because they've lost their joy.

But God, I know their joy has not really been lost. You have been carefully holding it and protecting it for them, always offering to refresh them with it again. Singing is just another beautiful tool that releases it. A tool You have lavishly created that gives them the opportunity to engage with You again. To engage their joy again. To find hope again.

For those who previously loved to sing, thank You for speaking to them right now about this gift. It is an essential part of their bounce. A part of them has wanted to sing again, but they've been discouraged. Refresh their desire, and give them a renewed dose of joy, right now, as they sing.

Today, enliven their voices and their spirit.

Thank You for thinking of everything that we would ever need for resilience.

THINK AND PRAY

How would (or did) singing uplift your soul today?

What role might music and singing have in your journey to bounce forward?

How do you feel about a thirty-day challenge to keep worship music going in the background of everyday life? What do you think will be some benefits?

Make my prayer your own.

 # ADAPTIVE PROCESSING GIFTS

Emotions can be intense. Sometimes overwhelming. Maybe you've recently discovered something that has rattled you. You're disappointed. Angry. Scared. Confused. Uncertain about how to respond.

You're not alone.

We've all received heart-wrenching news. We might have preferred a literal punch in the gut. **But there's help in unexpected places today.** And you don't have to do anything to earn that help. In fact, you can't even *reject* that help. It's coming for you, whether you ask for it or not!

God has placed within us primal physical processes that help us move through painful emotional experiences. They are automatic processes, which means He is going to use these physical processes on our behalf, regardless of whether we are mindful of them or grateful for them. Much like our physical wounds are involuntarily healed with a scab, our emotional wounds are tempered by processes out of our control.

Today, let's consider two of these processes: breathing and REM sleep.

Breathing isn't something we choose to do. It just happens. I'm breathing as I type this, and you're breathing while you read this. Typically, we don't even think about this automatic process until we're reminded of it (like I just reminded you). Though we have the freedom to never pay attention to our breathing, being mindful of this automatic process and then calming our breathing with slow, deep breaths can lower our pulse and blood pressure and regulate our emotions. What an amazing gift of healing!

Additionally, in ways that are mysterious even to those who have studied brain functions, God seems to use rapid eye movements in our sleep to facilitate adaptive processing. This experience in our sleep explains why we may sometimes go to bed struggling with a situation but wake up with a slightly different perspective or decreased emotional intensity. Another amazing, and free, gift of healing.

Breathing and sleeping are non-returnable gifts **from our Creator!** Even if we reject Him, we can never reject these tools that He has given us. We can't physically refuse to use these tools. They are passive tools designed by our loving Creator and given freely to us!

PONDER THAT!

Today, practice being mindful of the automatic process of breathing.

Breathe in, slowly and deeply, while reflecting on God's love, power, and care. Remind yourself that He sees you. He knows.

Now, breathe out, imagining your destructive thoughts and the tension in your body being released. Never to be welcomed back.

Did you notice the shift in your thoughts? The calming of your body? What a beautiful, automatic gift!

Now, practice being mindful of your other automatic process, REM sleep. Tonight, remind yourself that God has orchestrated your brain to assist in processing and regulating your challenging emotions. REM sleep is a gift He's given you, a tool that requires no effort on your part. As you lie down to sleep tonight, embrace the God who will touch your tender wounds and fears while you are in your subconscious sleep state. You need only be still. Rest in knowing God is working on your behalf in ways you are unaware.

Allow yourself to be mesmerized by God's loving design of your brain and body, which allows you to cope more effectively with the thoughts and emotions you are experiencing today. Be in awe today as you ponder how God was creating these adaptive processes for you in the womb all those years ago.

Because He cares about what you are going through *right now*!

Thank Him for these good and perfect gifts!

VERSE OF HOPE

Every good gift and every perfect gift is from above, coming down from the Father of lights, with whom there is no variation or shadow due to change. —*James 1:17*

MY PRAYER FOR YOU TODAY

God, I pray for my friends who are reading this devotion today.

I pray they feel Your love and care as they ponder the automatic processes You created in their bodies to assist in their healing.

Right now, as they take a breath, make them aware that their
breathing can bring calm to their minds and bodies.
I pray You will calm them.

And, as they contemplate the impact of REM sleep tonight, I
pray that You will increase their trust in You. That they will feel
assured that You are an amazing Creator and that You desire for
them to be free from the agonies that could keep them stuck.

Father, thank You! You have given them everything they need!

THINK AND PRAY

What do you notice when you practice breathing deeply and slowly? What difference does it make for you emotionally and physically?

Take a few minutes right now to breathe in and think about God's love, forgiveness, wisdom, and strength coming into your life. Then breathe out and imagine
the lies of the enemy being eliminated.

When we're upset, especially for a prolonged season, our sleep is often one of the
first casualties. But it's really important. How are you sleeping these days? What
do you need to do to rest better at night?

Make my prayer your own.

 # FIGHT OR FLIGHT

I'll never forget the day. **The images, smells, and sounds forever etched in my memory.** I was the passenger as my husband drove on a country road in South Carolina. It was early in the morning, the air still cool and crisp. The truck in the oncoming lane ran off the side of the road, overcorrected, and suddenly began flipping uncontrollably in the air, coming toward us full speed!

There was nowhere to go. The glass particles from their vehicle landed on our windshield as the truck tumbled over the top of ours. Three teenage boys were being thrown around in the cab right in front of our faces.

Time was eerily slow in those crucial seconds. And there was nothing else in the entire world that captured our attention. We stopped near the truck. I ran quickly after my husband as he darted down the embankment. Both of us silently counting the boys on the ground, immediately aware that one was missing. We had clearly seen three young men tumbling in that cab. But there were no words. No time for words.

Like nothing I've ever seen before or since, I watched as my husband picked up the truck and flipped it back onto its tires, uncovering the third boy. An ER nurse who came on the scene right after us quickly took over.

My heart is racing right now as I retrace my steps. The images invade my mind as if this incident just happened just seconds ago. Gratefully, those three boys survived the crash, and we walked away with nothing more than remnants of shattered glass on our vehicle. After the shock wore off, I found myself struck by having watched my husband flip the car off that young man—and the supernatural strength that came from his arms and legs that day. How was that possible?

While I don't doubt for a moment the intervention of God and His angels that day, I also am aware of the physiological reaction of fight or flight, a response that God created in our bodies. A response with an active and productive purpose.

Fight or flight is a carefully designed physical reaction of the sympathetic nervous system in response to acute stress or danger. The result of a threatening circumstance is a cascade of symptoms that position the body to respond and survive. Hormones like adrenalin and cortisol rush through the body, and blood flow is directed to the brain, muscles, extremities, and senses, resulting in increased strength, heart rate, and awareness of surroundings. Fight or fight is a critical gift for situations like the car accident that we witnessed.

But sometimes we experience this kind of arousal when we aren't in the midst of a tragedy.

We're just watching one on a screen. Or having a thought about a catastrophic circumstance.

The body doesn't detect the difference between real or perceived danger, and the sympathetic nervous system is triggered to defend and protect, even during an imaginary threat. **When that happens, the response that's designed to protect us actually does us harm,** and we're left with a high heart rate, pale face, dizziness, dry mouth, tense muscles, dilated pupils, nausea, and trembling.

Panic attack!

PONDER THAT!

Today, consider times in your life when your fight-or-flight response has served you well. Thank God for designing your body to respond to acute danger involuntarily and effectively. Next, consider times when a catastrophic thought or flashback of a traumatic image has triggered a fight-or-flight response. Ask God to make you aware of times when you experience unnecessary suffering from this misplaced automatic response. The next time you experience physical symptoms of panic when you are not in a threatening situation, breathe deeply and assertively, and remind yourself that you're safe. Say it out loud. Notice the parasympathetic system reversing the cascade of symptoms that are bringing unwelcomed discomfort, and thank God for the calming that comes.

VERSES OF HOPE

And Moses said to the people "Fear not, stand firm, and see the salvation of the Lord, which he will work for you today. For the Egyptians whom you see today, you shall never see again. The Lord will fight for you, and you have only to be silent." —*Exodus 14:13-15*

MY PRAYER FOR YOU TODAY

God, I pray for my friends who are reading this devotion today.

May they be awestruck by Your ingenious and creative design of our bodies and brains. Thank You for the fight-or-flight response that works so beautifully and protectively when it's properly initiated in times of acute danger.

But give my friends wisdom about when a fight-or-flight response is triggered when there is no real danger, resulting in symptoms that may harm them.

Father, give them immediate awareness of any catastrophic thoughts or triggering media exposure so they can be grounded. So they can avoid unnecessary suffering, panic, or conflict.

So they can bounce!

THINK AND PRAY

When have you experienced a fight-or-flight response used effectively in the face of a threat?

When have you experienced this response while watching a movie or reading a book?

When have you experienced a fight-or-flight response when you thought about
a catastrophic event?

Make my prayer your own.

DAY 38 THE TEMPLE

We are so accustomed to thinking of a temple in terms of stone and mortar, but the temple where God dwells now, through the Holy Spirit, is in you and in me. So it's important to take care of our physical body. Because our body is not our own. It's a precious dwelling, possessed by God.

Our body is also a crucial piece in the puzzle of our mental health. Because God made us whole and complex beings, our physical health directly impacts our mental, emotional, and spiritual health (and vice versa). This crucial insight explains why sickness, hormones, vitamin deficiencies, and disease processes impact our emotional health. And while we certainly can't avoid all of the un-welcomed physical complications that we may face, there are two simple areas that we may more effectively manage, right in the comfort of our homes. Starting today.

God has designed our bodies with muscles and joints for movement and activity. Exercise is not just prescribed for many physical conditions; it's also good for our brains (and therefore our mental health).

God has designed our bodies to require food as fuel, and the food that He made for us (instead of chemically laden processed food) is medicinally good for our brains. Remember, the brain is an organ of the body, and anything that contributes to our overall physical health also contributes to our brain health (which then contributes to our mental health).

Much of our journey with mental health requires cooperating with God in His design for our physical, mental, emotional, and spiritual health.

PONDER THAT!

Today, focus on your physical body as a way of addressing your emotional health. Consider what you can do to take care of your body and your brain. Eat healthy meals and imagine how those foods are nurturing the health of your brain. Then take a thirty-minute walk, breathe deeply, and thank God for the gift of a body that was designed to move. Notice the lift in your spirit as a result of your movement as your mental health neurotransmitters release chemicals that soothe your symptoms and boost your mood.

VERSES OF HOPE

Do you not know that your body is a temple of the Holy Spirit within you, whom you have from God? You are not your own, for you were bought with a price. So glorify God in your body. —*1 Corinthians 6:19-20*

MY PRAYER FOR YOU TODAY

God, I pray for my friends who are reading this devotion today.

Give them eyes to see Your design of their bodies. Allow them to view Your design from Your perspective. To consider the purpose and gift of muscles and joints that allow them to move. Of a heart that pumps their blood.

Today, give them eyes to see Your design in creation, which provides medicine and fuel for their bodies through the food you have provided. No longer manna falling from heaven, but a luscious and colorful variety of foods with such amazing healing ingredients that it still baffles the minds of experts.

Increase their motivation today to take care of the only temple they will ever manage. Show them the people they need to help them manage the physical challenges they want to address.

Father, I pray You will honor their efforts to care for their bodies by allowing them to experience increased energy, reduced inflammation, improved confidence, and stable emotions. I trust their physical health will pay dividends in every other aspect of their lives.

THINK AND PRAY

What are your concerns about your physical health? In what ways, if any, do you feel weak or sick?

How are any physical challenges impacting your mental health?

If this is an area in which you feel you are stuck, whose help do you need in order to get started (your physician, a friend, a counselor, a nutritionist, a fitness coach, etc.)? What difference will it make to have people like this cheering you on?

Make my prayer your own.

 INVISIBLE EMOTIONAL BOUNDARIES

COVID is contagious. Not much debate about that. The flu, the common cold, a stomach bug. Also contagious.

In a different way, a yawn is contagious. You might be yawning right now at the sight of the word. It's not an infectious disease. But it's an infectious experience.

Even a belly laugh is contagious. Another infectious experience. Think about the last time you watched someone laugh hysterically. You know, the laugh that came from the belly and might have even created a snort or a bursting forth of their last sip of a drink. Regardless of whether it was a friend or a stranger, whether you were right beside them or across the room from them, you almost certainly started laughing too. You couldn't contain it. Because their laugh was infectious!

We're all acquainted with the variety of infectious diseases. They make sense and are commonly understood. But what's not so commonly understood is that **challenging emotions can also have a contagious effect.**

Consider how you feel when you spend a lot of time with someone who is anxious. You may begin to feel anxiety as well. If you spend a lot of time with someone who is deeply depressed, you may also begin to feel down. If you spend a lot of time with someone who is bitter, you may also begin to feel tension and resentment.

If you are struggling today, pause to consider the emotional state of those with whom you spend most of your time. It's possible that your symptoms bleed into one another. Since mental health symptoms can be strangely contagious, you might not just be having your own symptoms today. You may also be experiencing the contagious effect of someone else's anxiety. Someone else's depression. Someone else's anger.

And someone you care about may be experiencing the overflow of your symptoms. Be alert to emotional contagions, an insight that can motivate you to make good choices today!

PONDER THAT!

Visualize the "shield of faith . . . the helmet of salvation . . . and the sword of the Spirit," which protect your mind and emotions from your unseen spiritual battles. Embrace what I call *invisible emotional boundaries* as you discern the line where someone else's thoughts and emotions end and yours begin. When you determine that a friend or family member is experiencing a strong emotional response, evaluate any contagious effect, rest in a passage of Scripture that speaks truth to your situation, and embrace God's protective boundaries over your mind. Thank God that you can stand firm mentally as you love and support your loved one through their challenges.

VERSES OF HOPE

In all circumstances take up the shield of faith, with which you can extinguish all the flaming darts of the evil one; and take the helmet of salvation, and the sword of the Spirit, which is the word of God, praying at all times in the Spirit, with all prayer and supplication. —*Ephesians 6:16-18*

MY PRAYER FOR YOU TODAY

God, I pray for my friends who are reading this devotion today.

You've created so many mysterious things, and a contagious effect is one of them. God, I pray You'll protect my friends from contagious infectious diseases that create physical challenges.

And I also pray You will protect my friends from contagious infectious experiences that create emotional challenges.

Give them wisdom about how to use this infectious effect in a powerful and healing way by surrounding themselves with people who are emotionally and spiritually healthy. And give them discernment about any symptoms they're having that are "caught" from the exposure to someone else's anxiety or depression that's weighing on them.

Give them invisible emotional boundaries that protect their minds and emotions from a negative contagious effect. And help them to have hope that's overflowing and contagious enough to spread to others who also need a bounce.

THINK AND PRAY

What do you notice about how the excitement or enthusiasm of others affects your mood and outlook?

What do you notice about how the sadness, anxiety, or anger of others impacts your emotional well-being?

Where might you need to incorporate invisible emotional boundaries? What would that look like? What will be some of the benefits?

Make my prayer your own.

Are you feeling drained today? Are relationships further complicating your emotional well-being? Do you spend time with your friends with hopes of feeling better, but you feel even worse afterwards? Are your friends also struggling in ways that prevent them from being able to influence you in a healthy way?

Are your relationships fertilizing your depression? Making you even more anxious? **That's because our closest relationships have a tremendous influence on our emotional and spiritual health.** Relationships matter.

It's true. Jesus was drawn to troubled people. But He never let them lead Him. He had great compassion for the troubled people who surrounded Him, but He never depended on them for emotional support. Even more importantly, His time with the Father far outweighed His time with broken people. And His Father was always with Him and in Him.

If you're wrestling with confusion and challenging mental health issues, it's important to evaluate your influences. Who do you spend your time with? Who counsels you? Whose ear do you bend? Whose words have the most influence in your life?

These are crucial questions, because struggles are contagious, and because the influence of others shapes our moods, our emotions, and our responses to the people and situations we encounter every day.

PONDER THAT!

Today, conduct an influence audit. Who has the most influential impact on your thoughts, emotions, and responses to life? Are you satisfied with your answer? If so, consider yourself blessed and praise God right now for placing that person in your life. This person is a source of light and encouragement, and you function better because of this relationship.

However, if your audit exposes some concerns, if you notice that the people who influence you the most actually weigh you down, then reconsider the impact of these relationships. A person who is captured by their strongholds of sin, or a person who is oppressed by their own mental health crisis, is not capable of providing you with a stabilizing influence. An influence audit, with appropriate adjustments, may allow you to be strengthened "like a tree planted by streams of water that yields its fruit in its season" as you spend more time with wise, secure people (Psalm 1:3)

VERSES OF HOPE

Blessed is the man
who walks not in the counsel of the wicked,
    nor stands in the way of sinners,
nor sits in the seat of scoffers;
    but his delight is in the law of the Lord,
and on his law he meditates day and night.
    He is like a tree
planted by streams of water
    that yields its fruit in its season,
and its leaf does not wither.
    In all that he does, he prospers.
—*Psalm 1:1-3*

MY PRAYER FOR YOU TODAY

God, I pray for my friends who are reading this devotion today.

I pray that You will reveal the influence of the people in their lives. Reveal the relationships that encourage wisdom and mental health.

And reveal the relationships that are preventing their bounce.

You created us to live in community with one another, sharpening one another as iron sharpens iron, and having roles of friend, mentor, or mentee. Give my friends wisdom regarding their roles in their relationships, particularly those with the most influence (good or bad). Give them insight to see clearly any area where they are being led by someone who is causing them to stumble.

Bless them in their influence audit and give them the wisdom to make any adjustments. Protect them from toxic relationships, and shift their dependence to You as they seek to be unstuck and continue moving forward.

THINK AND PRAY

List the five people you spend most of your time with.

How does each one influence your mental health? (Be ruthlessly honest.)

How do they influence your relationship with Christ?

How do those people either encourage or hinder your bounce forward?

Make my prayer your own.

WALKING ON EGGSHELLS

Are you walking on eggshells? Afraid of saying the wrong thing? Afraid of doing the wrong thing? Afraid of making the wrong decision? Afraid of upsetting someone? **Afraid of the next criticism, outburst, or silent treatment?** Hypervigilant. Fearful. Experiencing chronically tense muscles and upset stomach. Pretending to be okay, in a desperate effort to cope.

Queen Esther understood. She had to walk on eggshells around a king who was unpredictable, a womanizer, possibly an alcoholic, who sometimes gave the death sentence for those who came into his presence uninvited, and who loved to throw lavish feasts so he could be the center of attention. Not the most approachable guy. Perhaps even narcissistic.

Given that data, Esther's walking on eggshells would have been a **normal response to her situation.** Everyone around King Xerxes probably walked on eggshells. Nervous. Uncertain. Trying to please.

Today, you may be feeling like Esther. You live with hypervigilance. Easily startled. Avoiding certain situations or conversations. Trying to make sure everything is perfect in an effort to prevent a critical response from someone close to you.

You can't forget situations when things didn't go well. **You see the images in your mind right now.** And you never want to experience that again.

Esther could relate to that oppression. That nervousness. Normal mental health symptoms amid challenging circumstances.

But Esther had the wisdom to pause. To step back and evaluate her situation. With objectivity gained from this pause, she was able to see the dynamics of her situation more clearly. With the guidance of her mentor and the prayer support of a few close friends, she developed a logical strategy to address her situation and confront the person whose consequences she feared most.

PONDER THAT!

Are you in a relationship that leaves you walking on eggshells? Take the hand of a trusted mentor, pastor, or counselor, and give yourself the gift of that person's objective evaluation. Step back and observe the dynamics of your situation as if it were not your own. As if you were looking through the window into another person's life. Is your emotional response minimized based on an objective evaluation of your situation? Is your emotional response exaggerated? Or does your emotional response fit, given the hard realities you face?

Is your nervousness a normal and healthy response to an oppressive relationship dynamic? Are you emotionally and/or physically unsafe right now? Or is your current relationship safe, and your hypervigilance due perhaps to an unresolved, previous trauma?

Evaluate your experience of walking on eggshells and the data that your emotional response is providing. Then, with the prayer support of a couple of trusted friends and the leadership of someone spiritually and professionally qualified to guide you, develop a strategy that allows you to effectively address your situation and your emotional responses.

*If you determined today that you are in an unsafe situation, and you want to better understand your resources, call 9-8-8 for immediate assistance.

VERSES OF HOPE

And when the king saw Queen Esther standing in the court, she won favor in his sight, and he held out to Esther the golden scepter that was in his hand. Then Esther approached and touched the tip of the scepter. And the king said to her, "What is it, Queen Esther? What is your request? It shall be given you, even to the half of my kingdom." —*Esther 5:2-3*

MY PRAYER FOR YOU TODAY

God, I pray for my friends who are reading this devotion today.

Some of their relationships are life-giving,
calming, and stabilizing.

But some of their relationships may be threatening their mental health. Some of my friends may be in a toxic relationship that's triggering symptoms of anxiety. And until right now, they didn't make the connection between their challenging relationship and their mental health symptoms.

Father, for my friends who are walking on eggshells, I pray that You will give them discernment. I pray You will show them who they can trust to talk about this. And I pray You'll give them the courage to reach out for guidance.

Thank You, God, for revealing truth, and make clear any conversations, adjustments or boundaries that are needed. Even though it's hard and messy at times, thank You for the bounce!

THINK AND PRAY

How many days in an average week are you walking on eggshells?

If you report more than one day of every week, in what setting(s) are you most likely to experience these symptoms? (work, spouse, children, parents, neighbors, etc.)

Who do you know who can give you some trusted, objective, and godly guidance about your situation?

Make my prayer your own.

You may be wrestling with a broken relationship. The separation breaks your heart. You feel like you aren't being heard. The other person probably feels the same way.

Some days, it's all you can do to hold it together. The division hurts and is causing a significant amount of emotional turmoil. You just want things to be better. But you don't know how.

"Emotional intelligence" is the ability to regulate emotions, effectively communicate, manage conflict, and bounce back from criticism or failure. Many experts believe that emotional intelligence is more important than academic IQ in determining how successful a person will be at navigating life. **At the root of emotional intelligence is empathy, an underrated but essential ingredient for successful relationships.**

Empathy is the ability to imagine yourself in the circumstance of another person, to feel what they might be feeling, given everything that you know about them and the context of their situation. Empathy requires significant intention, concentration, and effort.

Empathy isn't easy. And it's not comfortable. But empathy is a fundamental necessity for healthy relationships. If we want to get along with others, we must seek to understand why they think, feel, and act the way they do.

One of the essential ingredients of counseling is empathy. If I cannot *fully immerse* myself into the hurts, thoughts, and emotions of another person, then I am *unable to* facilitate the journey to healing. Yes, this empathetic immersion requires a sacrifice of time, attention, and emotional space. For me, it has also been the sacrifice of decades of exposure to secondary trauma, that is, the trauma other people tell me about.

I won't pretend to suggest that the sacrifice is easy. It isn't for me, and it won't be for you. **But healthy relationships are impossible without empathy.** Marriage relationships. Parenting relationships. Church relationships. Community relationships.

So where do we start? **Speak less. Listen more.** Most of the time we live as if we had two mouths and one ear. But *God created us with two ears and one mouth.* So, start by listening. Listening to discover and understand. Listening with intention and concentration. And then asking clarifying questions to make sure you are understanding correctly. When you give someone a gift of being heard and understood, you have given a gift of healing.

But let me give a word of warning: If the person is abusive or threatening in any way, your compassion may need to come from a distance. It's not wise to expose ourselves to unsafe people. When possible, lean in toward the process of forgiving and reconciling, but when that's not possible, forgive but stay safe.

PONDER THAT!

A relationship in your life may need healing. Let empathy fan the flame! For the next twenty-four hours, implement what I call a "typical day exercise." Intentionally imagine life from the perspective of this other person. Consider the situations they might face today, from the time their feet hit the floor until their head meets the pillow tonight. Imagine the fears, responsibilities, stressors, hopes, interactions, challenges, and vulnerabilities they may encounter. Consider the emotions they may feel. Allow yourself to be fully immersed and seek to understand their perspective. Be sure to take some notes about what you observe.

VERSE OF HOPE

Finally, all of you, have unity of mind, sympathy, brotherly love, a tender heart, and a humble mind. —*1 Peter 3:8*

MY PRAYER FOR YOU TODAY

God, I pray for my friends who are reading this devotion today.

Today's devotion may have triggered grief regarding relational tensions and divisions. Lord, I pray You will use these emotional responses to make my friends thirsty for empathy. Even toward those who have wounded them and who have contributed to the fragile state of the relationships.

God, give them insights about why others may think, feel, and act the way they do. Guide them to sacrifice the time, attention, and emotional space it takes to experience empathy, even for their offender, knowing that empathy is an essential ingredient for healthy relationships.

Father, taper their speaking.

And fertilize their listening.

Reveal Your will for a release of the relationship when that's the only recourse, or a reconciliation of the relationship when the other person is willing.

THINK AND PRAY

What specific relationship(s) did today's devotion bring to mind?

Take twenty-four hours to do the "typical day exercise." Write down your list of observations.

How did God use this exercise to guide your steps?

Make my prayer your own.

 HELPER'S HIGH

Feeling stuck today? Lost in your racing thoughts? Consumed with your struggles? Fixated on your worries? Gripped by bitterness? Feeling helpless, hopeless, and worthless? You want to bounce forward, but you're not sure how to get out of the pit!

Can you imagine being able to take a break from the unintended, overriding focus on yourself? Can you imagine becoming lost in the joy of serving another person, despite your suffering?

Think about the last time that you paid for the meal of a struggling stranger. Or surprised a lonely friend with a thoughtful gift. Or helped an elderly person in the grocery store. Or provided a listening ear and a word of encouragement to someone who was discouraged. Or patiently listened to a child. Do you remember the feeling of euphoria that followed your kindness?

That euphoric feeling was no coincidence. **That "helper's high" was an unexpected gift of God to jolt your bounce forward.** Due to a chemical release of neurotransmitters and hormones, our brains respond positively when we serve others. A genuine and natural sense of happiness and satisfaction results from assisting others. God designed our brains to reward us with this natural high when we take our eyes off ourselves and serve others. The result is a beautiful cascade of emotional and physical relief that ministers to us in our own pain, and gives us a welcome dose of hope.

Acts of selflessness don't minimize our struggle or pain. They just shift our perspective.

Kindness towards others in need reminds us that everyone has trials and hurts. We aren't alone. God can use our messy seasons to be a blessing to someone else. Despite our own suffering, our ability to lend others our presence and care is still intact.

In Scripture, we see the ultimate example of selfless serving in suffering. The day before His crucifixion, Jesus served. Anticipating the darkest day of His life (and of history), Jesus could have withdrawn from His followers. Or He could have insisted that they serve Him. Instead, Jesus washed the feet of His disciples and served them a meal. **It wasn't a convenient time. Emotionally, He faced the greatest turmoil anyone had ever encountered. But Jesus leaned in. He took eyes off himself and His own suffering and served humbly and magnificently.** And because He was human, I can only assume that Jesus felt the relief and contentment that followed these selfless, sacrificial acts. Jesus may have experienced the invisible blessing of a "helper's high" the day before He died on the cross for you and for me. A blessing that kept Him focused on His why, jolting forward to His undeserved death, with a relentless love for the undeserving and the ability to give the gift of salvation to a lost, lonely, and dying world.

PONDER THAT!

As you move through your day, look for someone who has a need. Maybe the need is physical. Maybe it's financial. Or emotional. Or spiritual. Allow yourself to take a break from your own pain as you care for another person. Notice the emotional and physical effect you experience, and thank God for the unexpected gift of the helper's high that gives you perspective . . . and puts a little bounce in your step.

VERSE OF HOPE

Now before the Feast of the Passover, when Jesus knew that his hour had come to depart out of this world to the Father, having loved his own who were in the world, he loved them to the end. —*John 13:1*

MY PRAYER FOR YOU TODAY

God, I pray for my friends who are reading this devotion today.

I trust that You will put someone in their path today who needs some help. I pray You would give my friends Your eyes to see this opportunity. I pray You would prepare their schedules and their hearts to be interrupted and inconvenienced. And I pray that tonight, when they look back on this day, they will be able to see the blessing You provided of being able to help another person.

I pray they would enjoy the respite from their own heartache and experience the slight euphoria of focusing on the hurts and needs of another person, not just their own pain.

Father, I pray that as my friends reach out to others in need, You would refresh them. Allow the temporary relief from their pain to launch them toward hope with another bounce forward!

THINK AND PRAY

If you're starting your day, where might you encounter someone you can help?

If you've taken this step today, what was your response after helping someone?

Emotionally:

Mentally:

Physically:

Spiritually:

How did your focus on their struggles and needs shift your perspective about your own struggles and needs?

Make my prayer your own.

   # MADE TO SOAR

Eagles are fascinating, awe-inspiring creatures. There is an eagle sanctuary in a theme park in Tennessee that I love to visit. In the 30,000 square foot aviary, you can see many bald eagles that can't be released into the wild because of an injury. And when you are that close to these marvelous animals, you can't help but reflect on the characteristics that make them so unique and special.

Though we don't see them very often in the wild, the presence of these spectacular birds is woven through Scriptures, and they are worthy of our reflection.

Eagles are like no other creatures. They have many unique qualities, but I'm especially impressed by how they respond to difficulty. Most animals, birds, and humans take shelter in a storm. But not an eagle.

Fearlessly, eagles fly into the storm and take advantage of the winds, which allow them to soar higher and faster. Talk about a bounce forward!

What a lesson for us! Instead of running from our life storms, we have the option of fearlessly embracing the strong winds, knowing they have the potential of producing something wonderful. Our life's storms can allow us to soar!

Today, you may be in a storm. You're trying to seek shelter, but there seems to be no protection. You're scared. Your emotions are unpredictable and overwhelming, and you don't know what to do. You're panicky, and you're running out of energy.

If so, consider the eagle, who just stretches his wings and soars. It's that simple. He doesn't have to exert any of his own strength. No flapping of wings. He calmly and courageously lets the wind do the work, creating a powerful updraft.

The eagle instinctively trusts its Creator. And it trusts the process of the storm to create an environment where it can soar!

PONDER THAT!

Let's think on those last two sentences again: *The eagle instinctively trusts its Creator. And it trusts the process of the storm to create an environment where it can soar!*

Take a few minutes to meditate on today's Verse of Hope. God loves His creation, and I'm sure He enjoys the bald eagle. But you are His masterpiece. This verse is not for an eagle. This verse is for you.

As you meditate on this verse, visualize yourself in the posture of an eagle. Imagine instinctively trusting your Creator as you face your current storm. Envision patiently waiting as your Creator uses the very storm that surrounds you to renew your strength. Only God can create such a miraculous process. And it's not just a process made for eagles. You were made to soar!

VERSE OF HOPE

. . . but they who wait for the Lord shall renew their strength;
they shall mount up with wings like eagles;
they shall run and not be weary;
they shall walk and not faint.
—*Isaiah 40:31*

MY PRAYER FOR YOU TODAY

God, I pray for my friends who are reading this devotion today.

God, inspire them as they consider the amazing bald eagle.
You created that bird for Your pleasure and as a picture of Your
process of renewal in the face of the storm.

Allow them to visualize You renewing their strength in today's
storm, creating an updraft to carry them along.

I pray You will give my friends the instinctive faith of an eagle.
The wisdom to know when to seek shelter. And the discernment
of when to face the storm with abandon.

As they maneuver trials of life over the years, I pray You will build
their confidence in Your mysterious process to produce more
resilience.

Only You can use their storms that threaten destruction to be
the very tools that strengthen them. That cause them to soar.
That are the momentum for moving forward.

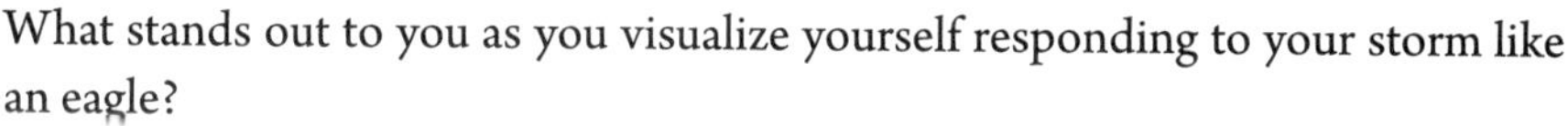

THINK AND PRAY

What stands out to you as you visualize yourself responding to your storm like an eagle?

What previous storms in your life have resulted in your being strengthened (emotionally, physically, mentally, spiritually, or relationally)? List some of those that stand out to you, and describe the specific strengthening impact.

Make my prayer your own.

DAY 45 — HIS NAME, ABOVE YOUR STRUGGLE

In the face of our pain, we sometimes fail to gain an accurate perspective. We tend to get tunnel vision when it comes to our heartaches. Sometimes, all we can see are our obstacles and wounds. Tunnel vision blinds us from being able to see the big picture. It prevents us from seeing the full truth.

What is the truth?

God is bigger than your depression.

God is more powerful than your anxiety.

God is triumphant over every physical, mental, or emotional struggle you have.

God's timing is often slower than ours, but He's always right on time.

There are many names for Jesus in the Bible: Christ. Emmanuel. Lord. Master. Lamb of God. Lion of Judah. Light of the world. Son of God. Savior. These are just some of the many beautiful names that represent the various characteristics of Jesus.

But every name of Jesus is above your present darkness. Every name of Jesus is above your depression. Every name of Jesus is above your anxiety. Above your loneliness. Above your self-doubt. Above your relationship strains. Above every struggle.

Stay there a moment. Let that sink in! **Call on His name! Worship His name! When you do, you are calling on the Person behind the name!** The Person whose name is above every other name!

Calling on Jesus will put your struggles in their place.

PONDER THAT!

Today, contemplate some of the names of Jesus. Write them down and reflect on their meaning. Consider how the different names speak specifically to the heaviness of your heart. Hold those names of Jesus above your present darkness and embrace the power of God, which is far greater and higher than your despair. Let His name be exalted, and call on Him to put your struggle in its place.

VERSE OF HOPE

Therefore God has highly exalted him and bestowed on him the name that is above every name. —*Philippians 2:9*

MY PRAYER FOR YOU TODAY

God, I pray for my friends who are reading this devotion today.

I exalt You, as the name above every other name.
There is no one like You!

Jesus. Christ. Emmanuel. Lord. Master. Lamb of God. Lion of Judah. Light of the world. Son of God. Savior.

I pray you will immerse my friends with knowledge of who You are. Overwhelm them with awe in Your presence. Allow the understanding of the fullness of Your character to give them confidence in the face of darkness.

What is depression to You, O God?

What is anxiety to You?

You are infinitely superior.

I pray You will birth in them an eagerness for resilience, knowing that You are the author of their bounce, and You eagerly want them to join You in being far above their struggle!

THINK AND PRAY

What name of God is most reassuring to you?

What does this name mean? And what does it speak to your situation today?

How do you feel about calling upon God for help today? How do you think He'll respond?

Make my prayer your own.

DAY 46 INDESTRUCTIBLE HOPE

Destructive storms. Destructive thoughts. Destructive relationships. Destructive habits. Destruction in our streets, and destructive wars in our world. We're exposed to destruction every day, and the damage chips away at *our hope*.

But, God . . . You see, the Word tells us that Jesus is the "indestructible life." Let that sink in! Jesus, who walked on this earth, had relationships and responsibilities. He experienced physical suffering and rejection. But He triumphed. He is indestructible.

Yes, Jesus is indestructible! His future is indestructible. His promises are indestructible. His love is indestructible!

He can never be annulled.

He can never be cancelled.

He is everlasting. Imperishable. Eternal. Immortal.

Permanent!

That means that I have a hope that is indestructible. Because my hope is in an indestructible God!

You have a hope that's indestructible! **Jesus will never be destroyed, and His care and power in your life can never be altered.**

PONDER THAT!

Today, when you wrestle with hopelessness, when you feel afraid, and when you worry about the future, remind your dark thoughts that your hope is indestructible! Draw close to Jesus. Sit for a while with Him today, meditating on the knowledge that He is your permanent anchor. Praise Him for being indestructible, for being your only constant. Meditate on this assuring characteristic of your Savior and Lord. Rest in His predictable presence and remind yourself throughout the day that He will always be there with you.

VERSES OF HOPE

This becomes even more evident when another priest [Jesus] arises in the likeness of Melchizedek, who has become a priest, not on the basis of a legal requirement concerning bodily descent, but by the power of an indestructible life. —*Hebrews 7:15-16*

MY PRAYER FOR YOU TODAY

God, I pray for my friends who are reading this devotion today.

I praise You, Jesus, for Your indestructible life. Your eternal presence, permanence, and peace.

You will never be erased, canceled, or removed.
You will always be!

I pray that my friends will find rest today in Your forever presence. That you will help them wrap their mind around what is mortally impossible. But immortally promised.

Give them assurance in your dependability
as they trust in You to lead them.

THINK AND PRAY

How does the truth of Jesus' "indestructible life" encourage you?

How can acknowledging the permanence of Jesus help you as you seek to bounce forward from a tough season?

Make my prayer your own.

DAY 47 HE CAME FORWARD

It's hard for me to study the details of the events leading up to and during the crucifixion of Jesus. It's emotionally overwhelming to consider the betrayal and cruel death of Christ.

Admittedly, I often skim over those Scriptures as quickly as I can, eager to just get to the resurrection. Hope is far easier to feel than sorrow or hopelessness!

Maybe you feel the same way. Especially if you are already feeling discouraged or sorrowful. **But** details matter. And there is a detail related to the death of Jesus that you and I need to see today. Because it changes everything!

We see a description of the events leading to the arrest of Christ in the eighteenth chapter of John. It is there that we learn that Jesus was in the garden, processing the heaviness of all that was to come. This specific olive garden was a place that Jesus frequented. In fact, John reported that He "often met there with his disciples," including His betrayer, Judas (vv. 1-2).

Jesus intentionally went to the place where He could most easily be found by those who wanted to kill Him. And when Judas showed up with an army to arrest Him, John reports that "Jesus, knowing all that would happen to him, *came forward*" (v. 1). He then invited the soldiers not just once, but twice to identify Him as the one they sought to arrest. Why twice? Because they "fell to the ground" the first time He identified himself (v. 6).

Jesus came forward. He made His arrest entirely effortless for His enemies. But there's more . . .

When Peter couldn't stand it any longer, he attempted to stop the arrest. He impulsively drew a sword and cut off the ear of Malchus, the high priest's servant. But Jesus' response only further demonstrated His determination to step toward His death. Jesus disciplined His defender, healed the ear, and reminded His followers and His enemies of the path that He was choosing to travel: "Shall I not drink the cup that the Father has given me?" (v. 11)

Jesus' enemies were not in control. Jesus' followers were not in control. **The only one in control during the arrest of Jesus was Jesus himself,** and nothing was going to stop the crucifixion from taking place.

Jesus allowed His own death . . . from the beginning until the finish. Neither His enemies nor His defenders could change His purpose. He embraced the betrayal. The suffering. The sacrifice. The unfairness of it all.

PONDER THAT!

Visualize Jesus walking toward His arrest, His eyes on you, resigned to make the only choice that could bring you hope. Today, ponder the radical love that "came forward" *toward* captivity so that you could experience freedom *from* captivity. He "came forward" so you could bounce forward.

VERSE OF HOPE

Then Jesus, knowing all that would happen to him, came forward and said to them, "Whom do you seek?" —*John 18:4*

MY PRAYER FOR YOU TODAY

God, I pray for my friends who are reading this devotion today.

Jesus, take them to Your crucifixion.

As uncomfortable as it is, take them there.

Show them Your posture. You came forward.

Give them eyes to see Your initiative toward the brutal sacrifice that would pay the penalty for their sins.

You came forward, *toward* captivity so that they could experience freedom *from* captivity.

You came forward so they could bounce forward. Allow that truth to sit deep in their souls, right now, fertilizing their hope and moving them through their suffering.

THINK AND PRAY

Today, what stands out to you regarding the posture of Jesus leading up to and during the crucifixion?

How are you responding, right now, to the knowledge that Jesus came forward for your sake?

Make my prayer your own.

DAY 48 TOLERATING THE MYSTERIES

Why? It's the most common question known to mankind. It's a normal question to ask, and it's perfectly okay to ask this question, particularly in the season of a significant loss or painful situation. This question has its place in our healing. But it can also become a toxic question. Because this question, of all the questions of our lifetime, is the one question most likely to keep us stuck, preventing our ability to bounce back from the hurts of life.

Simply put, camping out too long to try to discover "why" prevents resilience.

God has created us with inquisitive minds. We are inclined to analyze, research, and wonder. We *want* answers. Often, we feel we *need* answers. Sometimes we get stuck on a quest for answers, for some rationale for the pain that has intrusively invaded our lives. But in fact, some answers will never come on this earth, at least not in their fullness.

God has not only created in us a desire for answers, but He has also allowed seasons of mystery. We need to depend on Him whether we get answers or not. Our dependence during the uncertainties of life builds a bridge for faith, and it's the only sufficient landing place for our "why?"

Much of our maturity is developed from learning to tolerate the discomforts of life. Our emotional stability is developed as we manage the painful mysteries with healthy coping skills, instead of numbing and escaping.

If you're in a mysterious season today, it's okay to ask "Why?" Give yourself grace there. But be cautious about *clinging* to your "Why?" **The answers will likely be incomplete and will never be enough to satisfy.** They certainly won't be a source of hope.

Our hope is in the One who knows the answers to all our "Why's," and who clings close through our anxiety-provoking, sorrow-inducing, and mysterious trials of life.

PONDER THAT!

Today, normalize your tendency to ask "Why?" But also remind your doubts that your hope is in the One who holds the answer to your "Why?" Resist the urge to numb your season of mystery with a coping skill that will only intensify and complicate your suffering. And gently shift your query to a new question that will facilitate your bounce forward: **"What now?"**

VERSE OF HOPE

For the foolishness of God is wiser than human wisdom, and the weakness of God is stronger than human strength. —*1 Corinthians 1:25*

MY PRAYER FOR YOU TODAY

God, I pray for my friends who are reading this devotion today.

I pray they will find rest in knowing that You are perfectly wise, despite the glaring unknowns in their lives. I pray they will find strength in Your knowing what they cannot know. Calmness in Your perspective that they cannot fathom.

I pray they will be grounded in their knowledge of Your omniscience and trust Your love and power.

Father, I pray You will gently, lovingly, and patiently whisper the safety of a new question: "What now?" That You will allow them to hold their "Why?" with less intensity, and that You would allow them to hold uncertainty and hope in the same moment, right now.

Thank You for being present with them in the messes of uncertainty and struggle. Thank You for gently moving them forward, despite the mysteries.

THINK AND PRAY

You've experienced something painful. What are your "Why's"?

What answers have you already received?

How are you tempted to numb and leave unanswered the remaining mysteries that are so painful?

Recognizing that the answers may not come, are you ready to ask "What now?" What difference will this shift make?

Make my prayer your own.

If you are struggling emotionally, you may also be struggling spiritually. Doubt is our natural tendency during hard times. We tend to doubt God's care. It's a normal struggle. You aren't alone in your doubts, but the Scriptures are full of vital truths regarding God's care. So, let's take a look.

I invite you to read Acts, Chapter 7, before moving ahead with today's devotion. This specific passage describes the stoning of Stephen, and it's a powerful word that you may need to hear today.

After you've read the chapter, pay particular attention to verse 55, "But he, full of the Holy Spirit, gazed into heaven and saw the glory of God, and Jesus standing at the right hand of God."

Stephen saw Jesus standing at the right hand of God.

Standing. That may not seem very significant. But it is. **Because this is the only time the Scriptures indicate that Jesus _stood_ by the Father.** Every other time, Jesus is _seated_ at the right hand of God.

Jesus' posture of standing during the suffering of Stephen means something significant. Maybe He was standing in anger as He watched His child experience unjust suffering. Or standing with pride, like a standing ovation, because His child was finishing well. Or standing with arms open to welcome His child home.

While we don't know all that it means, Jesus' posture certainly implies that Stephen's suffering had His full attention.

Because Jesus cared about Stephen.

And Jesus cares about you!

PONDER THAT!

You may be feeling that God is distant, uncaring, or detached. You may feel that God is silent in a season in which you most need to hear from Him. Today, I want you to visualize Jesus _standing_ next to the Father, full of love. _His eyes are on you. You have His full attention._ Because He cares! Stay there a moment more. Take in that radical love and attentiveness. Don't rush away from this powerful and healing discovery. Jesus is closer than you think.

VERSE OF HOPE

But he, full of the Holy Spirit, gazed into heaven and saw the glory of God, and Jesus standing at the right hand of God. —*Acts 7:55*

MY PRAYER FOR YOU TODAY

God, I pray for my friends who are reading this devotion today.

I pray that You will allow them to be as moved by this Scripture as I am. Jesus, I thank You for Your loving care and concern, evidenced by Your standing next to the Father during the stoning of Stephen. I know that most of our communication is nonverbal, and I've never seen a more significant unspoken message. A message of attentiveness, care, and love.

God, I pray that my friends will experience Your attentiveness, care, and love in a very personal way today. And I pray that you will continue to reveal special truths in Your Word to encourage and equip them as they journey ahead in resilience!

THINK AND PRAY

Why do you think Jesus was standing as Stephen died?

What do you feel when you visualize Jesus standing next to the Father, with His eyes on you, fully attentive to your current situation?

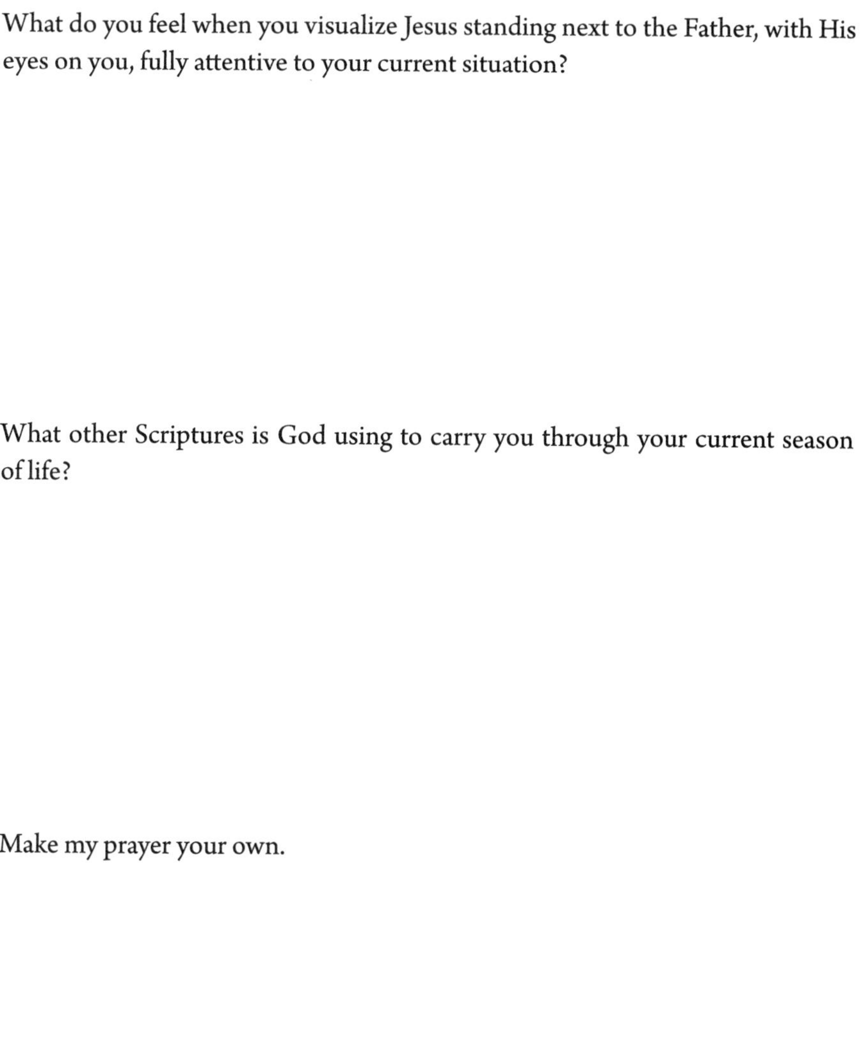

What other Scriptures is God using to carry you through your current season of life?

Make my prayer your own.

DAY 50   SINGING OVER YOU

Some days you wake up feeling that you don't matter. That you're insignificant. That you aren't good enough. That you have no meaningful contribution to make. That no one really cares.

Maybe today, the enemy is beating you with the whip of lies that you are unnoticed and unvalued. **Lies may sound good and right, but they're never true.**

Because you *do* have value. You *are* noticed. **You *do* have significance.**

God made sure His living Word included the most powerful image of His endearing love and enduring fondness for you. Your Creator *sings* over you! (Zephaniah 3:17)

He DELIGHTS in you.

The God of the universe rejoices over YOU.

He is with you *right now*. The one who has the power to save. He is with you. And it doesn't stop there!

He's not inactive in His presence.

He is celebrating over you. Elated. He is singing with gladness.

And this is no muted melody. This is not a bashful, hindered hum.

God's singing over you is loud, and His extravagant love can bring the quiet your soul desperately needs today.

PONDER THAT!

Today, rest in the image of God *delighting in* and *rejoicing over* you. Stay there. Breathe slowly and deeply. Stay there a moment more. *Take it in!* He has a crazy, radical love for you! Embrace the transforming reality of God's delight in you, even when your negative thoughts or emotions try to convince you otherwise. That powerful visual is ammunition in the battle of your mind and emotions. If you wrestle to visualize this and your dark thoughts won't allow you to accept God's love, reach out to a friend who will pray for you. Remember that Jesus is always praying for you. Ask Him to help you receive His delight over you.

VERSE OF HOPE

The Lord your God is in your midst,
a mighty one who will save;
he will rejoice over you with gladness;
he will quiet you by his love; he will exult over you with loud singing.
—*Zephaniah 3:17*

MY PRAYER FOR YOU TODAY

God, I pray for my friends who are reading this devotion today.

I pray they will experience Your presence and the assurance that they are seen, understood, and significant. Not only do You have the power to create them and save them, but You have the tenderness to sing over them.

Father, I pray the volume of your delight will refresh their souls and quiet the battle of their minds.

Thank You for announcing in Your Word that You delight in Your children. Unleash Your extravagant love and allow them to feel safe in Your love.

THINK AND PRAY

How did you experience the image of God *delighting in* and *rejoicing over* you?

Describe how this image challenges your perspective of God, and how it touches the longing of your heart.

If this image was challenging, it may be helpful to have a friend or mentor pray with you and for you. Who might you talk to about this?

Make my prayer your own.

DAY 51   SATAN'S ILLUSION

Today, you may feel that you are insignificant. Unseen. Unnoticed. Irrelevant. Worthless. Our toxic thoughts and painful emotions reinforce each other, and soon, it may seem like there's no way out. The lies we hear in our minds disarm us because Satan uses our own voices, our own thoughts, our own beliefs. These are false beliefs, but things we're sure are true.

It's such a convincing lie. It seems like there is so much "evidence" to back the destructive conclusion, and you often review that "evidence" in your mind. You reflect on your past. The demeaning words spoken over you. The rejecting glances of others. The painful dismissals from those you wanted to please.

But there is more to the story. **There's more to you. Because you *are* significant.**

Here's an important truth: The enemy, who can't steal your worth, can steal your *perception* of your worth. Read that again. Let it soak in. Satan is a vicious thief who robs you through an illusion. **And because *perception is reality*, the illusion still has the power to create an enormous amount of mental turmoil.**

Perhaps the enemy is robbing you today. Manipulating you to believe a false narrative about yourself. Remember, the enemy is an accuser. An exaggerator of lies. A minimizer of truth. A deceiver.

A liar.

Friend, Jesus was bold and unapologetic about defining himself. When falsely accused, He firmly declared that He was the "I Am" or "The Son of Man" or "The Light of the World." *Jesus didn't allow anyone or anything to define Him.* He boldly refuted and authoritatively corrected lies and attacks on His identity.

No one defined Jesus.

Jesus defined himself.

And He longs to define you.

PONDER THAT!

Let His affirmation in today. Let God speak truth over you. He has something to say, right now. Jesus longs to define you! If you are His child, believe Him when He defines you as His "masterpiece" (Ephesians 2:10). You are significant. You have incredible worth! Your freedom was so valuable to God that you were bought by the sacrifice of Jesus! His healing words will rescue your identity, free you from insecurities, and release you from the illusion of worthlessness that has plagued you. Today, ponder these words of truth regarding your significance, and let those truths play out in your mind like a movie. Go ahead, soak in the new evidence about your worth. Do that right now. Stay there for a few moments more and meditate on those truths.

VERSE OF HOPE

When Jesus spoke again to the people, he said, "I am the light of the world. Whoever follows me will never walk in darkness, but will have the light of life." —*John 8:12*

MY PRAYER FOR YOU TODAY

God, I pray for my friends who are reading this devotion today.

You know how they often wrestle with thoughts of inadequacy. With feeling they just aren't enough. Some days *feeling* they are invisible. Some days *wishing* they were invisible.

Satan has deceived them into believing that they are worthless.

God, meet them there, in their false beliefs. Please speak the truth so loudly that they cannot deny it. Give them the courage to allow You to be the only voice that defines their identity.

Father, fill them with Your Spirit, and rescue them from the illusion that they are insignificant.

I know that when You see them, You see the amazing creation You crafted. You love what You've made. They are so valuable to You that You sacrificed Your Son for their freedom.

I pray they would give You the stage to define them, right now. And that they would be energized with hope that pushes them along in their bounce forward today!

THINK AND PRAY

Write out three Scriptures that can serve as "new evidence" regarding your worth. (If you can't think of any, look at these: 1 Peter 2:9-10; Ephesians 2:8-10; and Isaiah 49.15-16.)

How do you think Jesus defines you? What words does He use? What conclusions does He draw?

What do you experience emotionally when you allow yourself to meditate on God's truth about you?

Make my prayer your own.

 # ON THE ALERT

If you are struggling with challenging physical or mental health symptoms, and you desire to be well, then you know what it feels like to be oppressed. As we open our hearts to hear God's words of affirmation, it's important to be aware of spiritual dynamics in our journey. So, let's talk about the oppression of spiritual warfare.

A child of God cannot be possessed by Satan but can certainly experience the targeted *oppression* of spiritual attack. Satan is threatened by any follower of God and opposes progress, freedom, and resilience. He wants you weak, discouraged, and confused. He wants you in chains.

If you are a child of God, Satan despises you. He hates you because he hates Jesus in you, and will use your emotional vulnerabilities against you. To keep you down. To keep you stuck. **To hold you hostage in a cage without bars.**

There are spiritual battles that are only seen in the spiritual realm but are felt in the physical realm. If we bury our head in the sand, or avoid the uncomfortable, uncertain conversations, we're even more vulnerable.

We can't afford to be naïve.

There's a war going on around us.

We have an enemy who takes advantage of our weaknesses, our genetic predispositions, our traumas, and our imbalances. He doesn't fight fair, and because of that, we need to be aware of his schemes and alert to our role in this spiritual battle.

PONDER THAT!

Read Ephesians 6:10-20 (which details preparation for spiritual warfare), and then visualize yourself as a soldier in battle. Consider your current situation and your vulnerabilities. Have you prepared for spiritual battle? If not, pray that God would reveal the insufficiencies in your preparation. It's time to "keep alert with all perseverance" and accept your warrior position, or complacency will be your biggest risk (v. 18).

VERSE OF HOPE

For we do not wrestle against flesh and blood, but against the rulers, against the authorities, against the cosmic powers over this present darkness, against the spiritual forces of evil in the heavenly places. —*Ephesians 6:12*

MY PRAYER FOR YOU TODAY

God, I pray for my friends who are reading this devotion today.

God, You allow the enemy to roam around on a short leash, and You allow the battles of the spiritual realm that interrupt our lives in our weakest moments. But I know that You are the final victor!

I pray that You will give my friends eyes to see their vulnerability and the schemes of the enemy.

I pray You will use Your Word as the only offensive weapon they need against the enemy. Draw them to Your Word, give them a love for the Scriptures. Give them understanding of Your Word as it applies to what they are facing.

Defend them with Your armor: with truth that gives discernment, righteousness that thwarts temptation, peace that allows them to approach others gently, faith that allows them to see beyond the invisible lies of the enemy, and the protection of their minds that sustains their stability. Remind them of Your constant presence and Your desire to connect with them throughout the day in prayer. Keep them awake and alert, guarding them from complacency. Give them strength to keep going, never quitting prematurely when the battle is still at hand.

Thank You, Father, for warning us about our enemy. I pray he will be the one held hostage as my friends continue in their journey of resilience.

THINK AND PRAY

What emotions do you experience when you study spiritual warfare?

What passages of Scripture soothe your concerns today?

In what ways do you believe you have experienced the oppression of a spiritual attack?

Make my prayer your own.

 # YOUR OFFENSIVE STRATEGY

There are many offensive strategies for mental health. Managing all aspects of the whole self requires a formulated plan, and you'll need to consult with a counselor, physician, and possibly a psychiatrist to develop a team approach to effectively manage the plan.

But the only offensive weapon for spiritual health is the Word of God (Ephesians 6:17). **And spiritual health matters.**

Meeting with God every day through His Word is a radically powerful and absolutely essential strategy. **So go ahead, obsess about Jesus.**

And do so unapologetically. He is your hope, and you can cling to Him throughout the day.

Every day.

Lean into the Scriptures. Meet with God in the morning, the evening, and as many times throughout the day as you need.

Don't beat yourself up if brain fog from depression prevents you being able to concentrate or to memorize passages.

Just keep going to Him, one verse at a time! And keep bathing in His love, His kindness, and His truth!

PONDER THAT!

Today, pick one meaningful passage of Scripture and write it on numerous index cards, placing them in your bathroom, your kitchen, your pantry, your car, your computer, and/or wherever you need a refresher of truth. Allow God's Word to ground you and help you regroup during moments of despair. Then, take the verse below, and meditate on it *one word at a time*. Close your eyes and soak in *every word*. Imagine yourself calmed by Jesus, accepting His invitation to unload your burden. His arms are a bed of rest for your weary soul.

VERSE OF HOPE

"Come to me, all who labor and are heavy laden, and I will give you rest."
—*Matthew 11:28*

MY PRAYER FOR YOU TODAY

God, I pray for my friends who are reading this devotion today.

God, thank You for Your Word. Our manual for living. Our one and only offensive spiritual weapon.

I pray You will give my friends a radical love for Your Word, so that when they study, You will draw them near. Give them understanding. Give them insights. Allow them to experience Your Word in an incredibly personal way today.

Father, You know that mental health symptoms make reading, concentrating, and remembering a challenge. I pray You will give them an extra dose of focus when they read, and allow them permission to take just one verse at a time if that's what works for them. Thank You for Your grace as my friends open Your Word and seek to find You there. God, I thank You that following You is not a performance. Your Word is how we commune with You, but it's not about how many verses we read or memorize in a day. Give my friends the freedom to read Your Word without worrying about being judged. And in that freedom, I pray they will dive deep, and that You will allow Your Word to become a powerful accelerant for their bounce!

THINK AND PRAY

What was your response in meditating on the Verse of Hope?

What passage is God using to carry you through your current season of life?

What tips have you discovered that help you to concentrate when you study the Bible?

Make my prayer your own.

 # INSTRUCT YOUR SOUL

Do you need stabilizing today? Do you find yourself frazzled, anxious, or uncertain about your future? Are you **paralyzed by analyzing your uncertainties**, as if it somehow solves the complex problems you face? Are your responses to the challenges of the day a reflection of your negative thoughts about the future? Are your behaviors influenced by your anxiety?

Though it rarely brings us joy in the moment, **God allows us some seasons of uncertainty.** Times in which we feel powerless. But we don't have to be passive.

In Psalm 103, we see David talking to his soul, directing himself to a state of mental, emotional, and spiritual grounding. **He beautifully commanded his soul to praise God "and forget not all his benefits."**

David didn't mention his prayers, his hurts, his disappointments, his traumas, or his requests. **Instead, he redirected himself entirely to praise.**

He instructed his heart to meditate on the characteristics of God to forgive, heal, redeem, love, and satisfy.

PONDER THAT!

While it's perfectly fine to petition God for your needs, I encourage you to instruct your soul to praise God for who He is and all He has done for you. Each time you think about the uncertainties of your present situation, instruct your spirit to praise God, focusing on the characteristics and blessings of God that bring you to a place of awe.

Today, practice redirecting yourself rather than passively allowing your thoughts to stay stuck on your pains and disappointments. Notice how this process of instructing your soul to praise shifts your thoughts, emotions, and even your responses to the challenges of the day.

VERSE OF HOPE

Bless the Lord, O my soul,
and forget not all his benefits.
—*Psalm 103:2*

MY PRAYER FOR YOU TODAY

God, I pray for my friends who are reading this devotion today.

They face some uncertainties that are triggering negative thoughts. And their negative thoughts are triggering anxiety. And anxiety is triggering some unhealthy and unhelpful responses.

God, help them to breathe deeply in Your presence, right now.

In this moment of calmness, help them stop focusing on their uncertain future, and give them the words to preach to their souls. Give them the wisdom to redirect their thoughts to praise. Like David, guide them to meditate on Your characteristics to forgive, heal, redeem, love, and satisfy.

Use this time of prayer and praise today to shift their thoughts and emotions and move them forward and restore their confidence in You.

THINK AND PRAY

What are your thoughts, worries, and feelings regarding your uncertain future?

What was it like to pause these thoughts for a short time today and redirect your soul to praise?

What are the specific characteristics of God that speak to your uncertainty and lead you to praise Him?

Make my prayer your own.

 # MY SHEPHERD

Imagine that you are a sheep. You're anxious. You're tired. You're stubborn. You're not sure what to do or where to go. Occasionally, you get stuck in a ditch. In the mud. You just feel overwhelmed.

Not too hard to imagine, is it? **Because we're all like sheep. And we struggle.** We need help. We need a competent shepherd.

Today, immerse yourself in Psalm 23. Don't just read the words. Stay there. Emphasize the personal application. *Treasure* these truths. *Meditate* on the words. *Visualize* the images. *This is for YOU!*

The Lord is **my** shepherd; **I** shall not want.

He makes **me** lie down in green pastures.

He leads **me** beside still waters.

He restores **my** soul.

He leads **me** in paths of righteousness

for his name's sake.

Even though **I** walk through the valley of the shadow of death,

I will fear no evil,

for you are with **me**;

your rod and your staff,

they comfort **me**.

You prepare a table before **me**

in the presence of **my** enemies;

you anoint **my** head with oil;

my cup overflows.

Surely goodness and mercy shall follow **me**

all the days of **my** life,

and **I** shall dwell in the house of the Lord forever.

PONDER THAT!

God has given each of us a powerful mind with the creative ability to meditate and visualize. When we visualize affirming truths, our bodies calm. When we meditate on encouraging truth, our minds calm. But when we're reckless with our powerful minds, our mental health symptoms escalate. The next time your symptoms threaten your functioning, go back to Psalm 23. Personalize David's words. Meditate. Visualize. And let the Great Shepherd comfort you.

VERSE OF HOPE

Your rod and your staff, they comfort **me.** —*Psalm 23:4*

MY PRAYER FOR YOU TODAY

God, I pray for my friends who are reading this devotion today.

They have probably heard this Psalm many times before.

But today, I pray You allow it to sit differently. To penetrate. To bring hope and health.

Ground them in knowing that You are their Shepherd.

Protecting. Comforting. Loving. Healing.
Providing. Leading. Preparing.

Now, in this very moment.

Give them awareness of Your presence. Encourage them.
Fuel them with hope!

THINK AND PRAY

How did you experience Psalm 23 today?

Which specific image was most powerful for you?

How does today's interaction with God's Word speak to the challenges you face today?

Make my prayer your own.

 # BETTER TO GIVE

If you've ever endured an emotional or relational storm in your life, you can appreciate how inwardly focused we can become when we struggle. We certainly don't mean to become self-absorbed, but our difficulties rope us in, and all we can see is our pain and suffering.

They monopolize our focus. Our thoughts. Our emotions.

We're vulnerable to a pity party. Even those of us who detest a pity party are susceptible under these conditions. We need a treatment for our self-absorption.

We need a solution for the tunnel vision that becomes nearly as destructive as our painful trial. At the risk of seeming too simplistic, I'll suggest a solution in a single word: *give*. Is it truly better to give than to receive? That's a generations-old cliché that deserves a little more attention, and you may not believe it until you try it. Only when you risk putting yourself in the position to give will you be blown away by the impact to your life.

Indeed, it's true that when we intentionally seek to meet the needs of others, we receive blessings in return. Our perspective shifts.

Our thoughts bounce away from our pain, and we experience an intangible joy based on our opportunity to bless others.

Those who reach out to others also gain the benefits of improved health, confidence, and diminished symptoms of depression and grief.

PONDER THAT!

Giving is the GIFT that keeps on giving! So give time. Give attention. Give thoughtful gifts. Give a smile. Give a compliment. Give a meal. Give a word of encouragement. Give a listening ear. Pay it forward, or just give back, and it will come right back around. Give, and you'll be glad you did! Take note of the shift in your thoughts and emotions when you give today, initiating a refreshing jump-start to your bounce forward.

VERSE OF HOPE

A generous person will prosper; whoever refreshes others will be refreshed. —*Proverbs 11:25*

MY PRAYER FOR YOU TODAY

God, I pray for my friends who are reading this devotion today.

I pray You will bring someone in their path today who has a need. Thank You in advance for the opportunity to give. Provide the physical, emotional, spiritual, and financial resources for them to give generously. Refresh them with the respite from their own pain and the shift in perspective. Thank You for the joy they will experience as they have the opportunity to participate with You in ministering to someone in need today.

Thank You for using them purposefully, even in the midst of their own demanding pain.

Thank You, Father, for the gift of Your presence. The gift of Your Son. The gift of forgiveness. The gift of purposeful living. The gift of hope. The gift of eternity with You.

Thank You for the gift of bouncing forward, as well as the methods and people You will use today to facilitate that process.

THINK AND PRAY

What are some of the consequences when your pain turns you inward and you experience a pity party?

Who is in your path right now who could benefit from your attention? Consider responding with a smile, a compliment, a meal, a thoughtful gift, or just a simple word of encouragement.

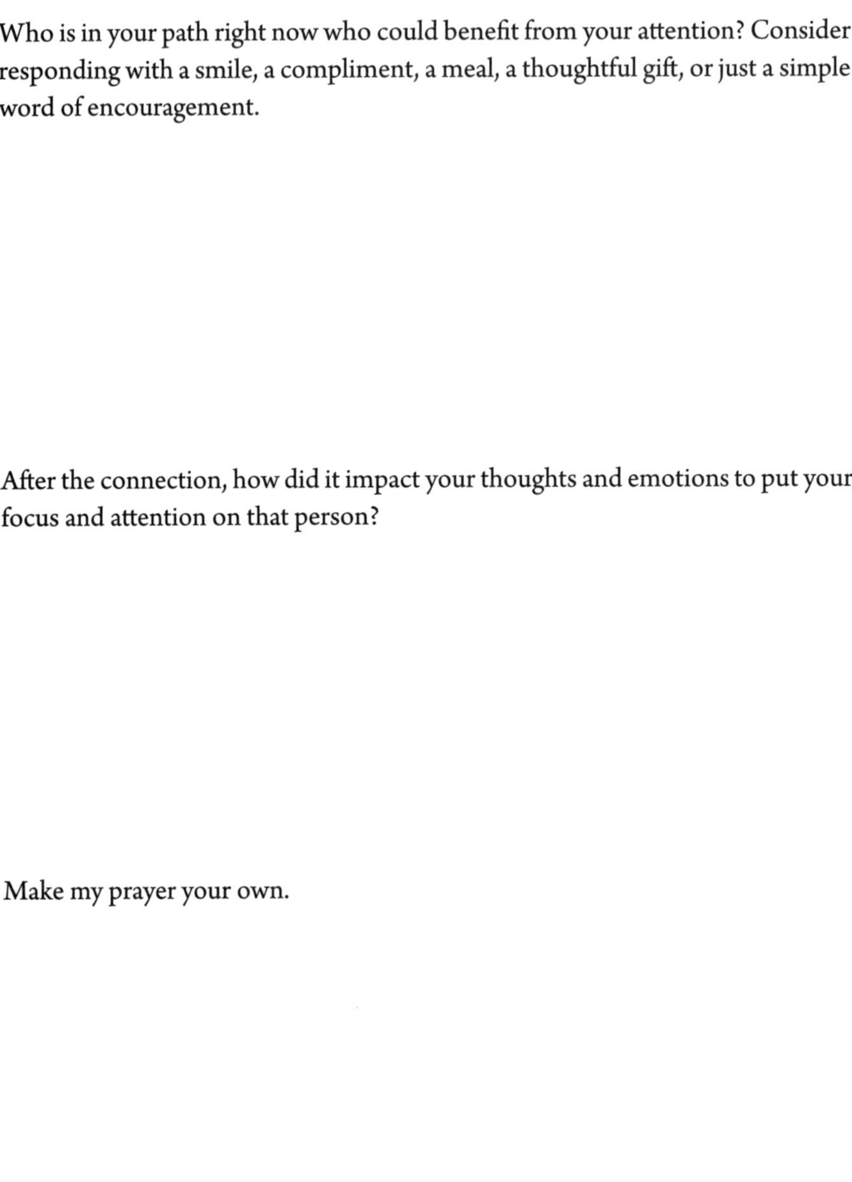

After the connection, how did it impact your thoughts and emotions to put your focus and attention on that person?

Make my prayer your own.

DAY 57 GRUMBLING AND GRATITUDE

We are so acquainted with our disappointments. Our minds naturally feast on the negative narratives of our frustrations. We repetitively rehearse our dissatisfaction.

Our thoughts easily shift to complaints.

We grumble.

We protest.

Sometimes silently.

Sometimes audibly.

Always with real consequences.

Our grumbling inevitably leads to discontent, and it's very easy for us to get stuck there.

The mind is poor at juggling both grumbling and gratitude. It seems that one starves out the other. Our ruminations regarding our complaints starve our ability to notice our blessings. Likewise, **our gratitude starves our negative thoughts.**

Gratitude is not just for the pleasant seasons of life. The Scriptures tell us to "give thanks in all circumstances" (1 Thessalonians 5:18). That means that today is a perfectly appropriate day for gratitude. **You can begin starving your negative thoughts, right now, with the vitamin of thankfulness.**

And since our thoughts influence our emotions, which then influence our behavioral responses, gratitude matters. **Gratitude is a prescription for mental health and can cascade love and strength into every other area of your life.**

Start by being thankful for the power of gratitude!

PONDER THAT!

Despite the frustrations and the circumstances that you face today, there are still opportunities to be thankful. And though it can sometimes be difficult to know God's will, we can be assured that it is *always* His desire that we give thanks. On tough days, it may seem that gratitude requires more creativity . . . and more determination. But even on our worst days, we can find something to be thankful for. Today, and each day for the rest of this journey, make it a point to notice, write down, and verbalize at least three things you are thankful for.

VERSE OF HOPE

Give thanks in all circumstances; for this is the will of God in Christ Jesus for you. —*1 Thessalonians 5:18*

MY PRAYER FOR YOU TODAY

God, I pray for my friends who are reading this devotion today.

Immerse them with reminders of Your blessings, large and small. Bring their grumbling to their awareness and use their gratitude as an antidote for their negative thoughts.

In the dark struggles of today, reveal things to praise. Fuel in them a habit of thanksgiving.

Gratitude is one of Your most powerful ingredients for resilience. Thank You for the blessing and power of such a simple tool. Let it not be far from their lips!

Father, thank You for steps of growth. Thank You for the encouragement. Thank You for the hope!

Thank You for the bounce!

THINK AND PRAY

What patterns of grumbling do you notice in your thoughts, now or over the past few days?

What three things are you grateful for today?

How will you remind yourself to develop the habit of gratitude?

Make my prayer your own.

 # WHERE RESILIENCE BEGINS

If you've made it this far, it's because you really want to bounce forward. You want to be whole. Healthy. Stable. *Resilient.*

You've been adding to your toolbox, taking note of emotional, physical, mental, and relational skills that will help you manage the inevitable challenges of your life. You're really trying hard, and you're probably noticing a shift in your thoughts, your emotions, and your responses to the circumstances of your life. You're starting to feel encouraged, and you're cautiously welcoming hope.

So it seems fitting, as we approach the close of this devotional, to make sure we go back to the beginning where resilience really begins. Our bounce begins . . . and ends . . . in the spiritual realm. **Because Jesus is the author of resilience.**

There are many aspects to our relationship with God and to spiritual disciplines. But the simplest, and most foundational ingredients for your bounce forward are confession and faith. According to the Scriptures, "If you *confess* with your mouth that Jesus is Lord and *believe* in your heart that God raised him from the dead, you will be saved" (Romans 10:9). And being saved isn't just a ticket to heaven; it's walking with God day by day.

If you want to thrive, first determine what you are going to do with Jesus.

Jesus has already been raised from death. And He is already Lord. But will you allow Him to be Lord of *your* life? Will you surrender everything? Even your pain? Even your purpose?

If you don't get this part right, it doesn't matter how many new tools you learn or how inspired you are by new insights. Without Jesus, you will only bounce so far.

PONDER THAT!

Consider the resurrection. Ponder the amount of power it would require for a person to be brought from death to life. That's supernatural power. The Spirit who raised Jesus from the dead is the same Spirit who lives within those who confess and believe. *The same Spirit,* with the same mind-blowing power to enable us to bounce forward from death to life! Jesus suffered the worst abuse, but

He came through it. And there's nothing you could face today that's overwhelming to Him. No trial in your life can overpower the Spirit of God within you. No stronghold is able to withstand His love and power. No despair is too dark for Him. No ruins are beyond His repair.

No sin is beyond His grace. No hurt is beyond His care. He's waiting. He's already paid the price for your redemption. And He's ready to help you recover, *His way*! If you've never surrendered to Jesus, today is your day. If you've walked away from Jesus, today is the day to come back.

Surrendering to His love, forgiveness, and purpose will change the trajectory of your life.

It's the only surrender that can ever propel you to *bounce!*

VERSES OF HOPE

But if Christ is in you, although the body is dead because of sin, the Spirit is life because of righteousness. If the Spirit of him who raised Jesus from the dead dwells in you, he who raised Christ Jesus from the dead will also give life to your mortal bodies through his Spirit who dwells in you. —*Romans 8:10-11*

MY PRAYER FOR YOU TODAY

God, I pray for my friends who are reading this devotion today.

They have been working really hard. Changing the way they think. Aware of their emotions. Seeking to make healthy decisions. Taking care of their bodies and their brains.

They really want to bounce. They thirst for resilience.

God, I know that You are the author of resilience.
And today, I pray that my friends will allow You to be
the leader of their resilience.

I pray that You will refresh the faith of my friends
who already know You.

And, I pray that faith would be birthed in my friends who have never known You. That today they would take the passenger's seat in their journey to bounce forward. You are already Lord.

But I pray that they would allow You to be Lord of their lives and the driver of their journey out of the pit. Thank You for hope, not just in the promise of heaven, but also in this life.

THINK AND PRAY

What decision you have made about Jesus?

Why have you made that decision?

What does it mean to surrender to Him? Does that scare you, confuse you, or excite you?

Think back to when you started this journey. In what ways are you moving forward in your bounce?

Make my prayer your own.

YOUR STRUGGLE GIVES BACK

It's hard to imagine how anything good could come from depression or anxiety. Or trauma or mental illness. Or the loss of someone you love. Or the death of a dream. Or from any other trial of life for that matter!

But God never wastes hardship. He never wastes a trial. He never wastes our pain.

In a way that only God can do, He allows our suffering to develop our strength! This is precisely why James suggests we meet our trials with joy.

That's a big ask! It's hard to meet depression or grief with joy, isn't it?

While it may be hard to be grateful for the hurt, it is possible to find gratitude for the fruit born from the pain! It's much easier to find joy in our extra dose of peace, or perspective, or kindness, or love. These are all fruits developed in us through the refining trials of life.

As Charles Spurgeon so beautifully recited, "I have learned to kiss the waves that throw me up against the Rock of Ages."

Unfortunately, our tendency is to look only at our pain. And we rarely embrace it. Far more often we want to run. We seldom even notice the victories that are born out of our trials.

But a look from this slightly different angle will serve us well. When we cooperate with God, even our suffering will bear the fruits of perseverance and perfection. "Complete, lacking in nothing."

That means our traumas and trials refine us and make us more like Jesus. From that angle, we can "count it all joy"!

PONDER THAT!

Today, ponder the fruits that have been born directly from your trials of life. How has your suffering given back? How have you become stronger, wiser, more compassionate? How have you learned who to trust and who not to trust? How has your pain matured you? Imagine how your life would be different, how you would be weaker, and how you would be lacking, were it not for the fruit you've realized as a result of your suffering.

VERSES OF HOPE

Count it all joy, my brothers, when you meet trials of various kinds, for you know that the testing of your faith produces steadfastness. And let steadfastness have its full effect, that you may be perfect and complete, lacking in nothing. —*James 1:2-4*

MY PRAYER FOR YOU TODAY

God, I pray for my friends who are reading this devotion today.

"Count it all joy" feels like an insult to their pain.
Like a command coming from a place
that lacks empathy or understanding.

And yet we know that James understood trials, physical pain,
injustice, unfairness, fear, loneliness, and loss.

I pray that You will bring forth a new understanding regarding James's challenge. An encouragement to look beyond the pain. To see the strength that is only born of suffering. The wisdom only born out of trials. And the empathy only born out of horror.

Father, fertilize the fruits that You desire to be born out of their hurt. Soothe their broken spirits as they see Your hand growing something beautiful in them. Something that they have always yearned for. Fruits like peace, perspective, kindness, and love.
Perseverance and hope—essential ingredients
of their bounce forward!

THINK AND PRAY

What is your emotional reaction to the words, "Count it all joy"?

Think of previous trials in your life. Which specific trials have had a positive im-pact on you? How have they made you stronger, wiser, and more compassionate?

Which previous trials of life are you now grateful that you experienced?

Make my prayer your own.

 # LOVED AND SENT

The disciples were disappointed. Disillusioned. They had hoped, but their hope was shattered. **Everything was different now.** They were scared. They were fearful of an uncertain future. Their response was completely normal, given the situation. **Because the One they had been following had just died on a Roman cross. And no one was expecting an empty tomb.**

But three days later, the unexpected happened. When Peter and John arrived at the tomb, they saw the facecloth set aside and carefully folded, and they must have gasped. **Hope returned. And everything was different now.**

In His grace, Jesus met the disciples where they were. In their thoughts and their doubts and fears.

Jesus spoke to Thomas's *doubting, hopeless, and destructive thoughts* in a physical manner, showing him His hands and His side. "Put your finger here, and see my hands; and put out your hand and place it in my side. Do not disbelieve, but believe" (John 20:27).

Jesus spoke to the disciples' *emotions of discouragement and anxiety* with His presence, "Peace be with you" (v. 21).

And Jesus spoke *guidance* with a challenge, "As the Father has sent me, even so I am sending you" (v. 21).

Jesus met them right where they were. In their mess. In their struggle. In their hopelessness. **In their thoughts, emotions, and behaviors.**

I trust He has done the same for you throughout this journey. My prayer is that your hope has returned, or at least is returning. And that you have encountered Jesus in the midst of your pain, your confusion, and your doubts.

If so, your thoughts are shifting. Your emotions are stabilizing. And even your actions have changed. You have hope! **Because when we meet Jesus in our mental, emotional, spiritual and physical messes, it changes everything!**

But it can't stop here. Hope is the most powerful and contagious experience we have. **But it's not to be hoarded!** Hope is to be given away.

PONDER THAT!

My pastor, Dr. Bruce Frank, often speaks of giving hope: "You are rescued, and now you are a part of the rescue team." If you've received hope, you become a source of hope for other people. Someone you meet today is struggling in their thoughts and drowning in their emotions. If you have hope today, then you have a rope to throw. *Hold on to Jesus, and throw the rope.* Just as my pastor concludes each service, I will give you the same reminder, "You are loved. And you are sent."

VERSE OF HOPE

Jesus said to them again, "Peace be with you. As the Father has sent me, even so I am sending you." —*John 20:21*

MY PRAYER FOR YOU TODAY

God, I pray for my friends who are reading this devotion today.

I am so grateful for the victories that You have orchestrated in their lives. For the growth and healing. For the shifts in their thoughts, emotions, and behaviors.

Thank You for hope! Thank You for their bounce!!

Now, Father, encourage them as they share their hope. Embolden them with the awareness of Your love. And send them to be agents of hope, pointing others to the Creator and the Author of their bounce!

Because hope is a person.

Resilience is contagious.

And a bounce cannot be contained.

THINK AND PRAY

What do you notice about your healing and growth as you look back over the last sixty days?

How have your thoughts shifted?

How have your emotions shifted?

How have your behaviors shifted?

Where do you see evidence of your bounce?

Who could use a bounce of their own?

Make my prayer your own.

Enjoy your bounce, my friend!

You are loved. And you are sent.

AFTERWORD

You made it!

Sixty days later, I hope you are seeing some improvement in your mental health and feeling some encouragement in your heart. I trust you've experienced some movement in your bounce forward! Thank God for that. He is the author of your bounce, and He provides every tool that pushes you toward hope!

Thanks for letting me be a part of your bounce! Now it's time for me to hand off the baton. So, continue your pursuit of resilience, persevere through the challenges, keep using your new tools, and stay connected with your brothers and sisters in Christ.

Be sure to share your story with a friend who needs some hope, because resilience is a gift that is waiting to be given!

Please note, this devotional is not intended to be a substitute for professional help, so if you notice that symptoms that you previously thought were temporary struggles are continuing to linger or worsen, then it may be time to reach out for help. If symptoms are interfering with your daily functioning, it is definitely time to reach out for help. If you are having thoughts of harming yourself, then it is vital that you reach out for help today.

There is hope. There is healing. But you may need some assistance from someone who is especially trained to facilitate your personal journey. No need to linger. Take courage. *It's time for your bounce forward, my friend!*

**If you are in need of immediate assistance,
contact the Suicide and Crisis Lifeline at 988.**

988lifeline.org

ACKNOWLEDGMENTS

I am grateful to God for gently loving me with truth and grace, and for crafting my heart with compassion for those who hurt. It is from this gift of compassion that I write. I am grateful for Jesus, who knows radical suffering and resilience, and who gave himself sacrificially for me. Every day that passes I grow more aware of my unworthiness of His great and generous gift. And I am grateful for the Holy Spirit, who guided me to pen the words of this devotional. If there is anything helpful in these pages, it can surely be attributed to Him.

Thank you to my husband, Mark, and to my children, Jordan, Joshua, Jacob, and Jeremiah: my five dearest brothers in Christ. God has used you to sharpen and challenge me. I am grateful for the conversations, the hikes, the many meals, the disagreements, the laughs, the trials, the celebrations, the ballgames, and every ounce of life that God has allowed me to share with you! Mark, you are the most faithful person I've ever met, and the biggest cheerleader behind my writing and speaking. Thank you for loving me so well!

Dr. Tim Clinton, thank you for having the vision for this devotional and for leading so effectively and creatively as pastors, counselors, and coaches around the world meet the mental health challenges of our time. Jennifer Ellers, thank you for your perseverance and patience, and the friendship that has been born out of the process of birthing this manuscript. I look forward to many more chats in our future.

Pat Springle, you are a gift! I am grateful for your encouragement and your thorough and efficient editing contributions. Your attention to detail is refreshing! Thank you for humbly sharing your publishing expertise and generously sharing your heart for those who are suffering.

Thank you to the Summit Wellness Centers team. You are the most gifted group of clinicians I've ever met, and I consider it an honor to serve alongside you. I have learned so much from you, and I am encouraged every single day as I watch God use you to facilitate resilience in individuals, marriages, and families. You are changing the world one person at a time!

To my clients, previous and current, I am grateful that God would allow me a front row seat as you trust Him for your bounce. I've learned my greatest lessons from those of you who trusted me in the trenches of your journey. Were it not for those sacred encounters, I'd have no expertise from which to write.

ABOUT THE AUTHOR

Donna Gibbs is a co-owner of Summit Wellness Centers, PLLC, and provides real HOPE and practical HELP for life's HURTS through the venues of professional Christian Counseling, writing, speaking, and consulting. Donna is the author of numerous book releases, and her blogs, devotions, and articles have frequently been shared in various media outlets. Among others, she has been a guest author with Ann Voscamp, LifeWay, Focus on the Family, PastorResources.com, YouVersion—Bible App, and American Association of Christian Counselors. Additionally, her creative and practical words of instruction and encouragement have been featured on many stages, radio broadcasts, and podcasts, including In the Market with Janet Parshall, Faith Radio, Moody Radio, Pat Williams Power Hour, Scripture Awakening, Prayer on Purpose, Billy Graham Evangelistic Association, Cross Rhythms UK, and She Works His Way. A member of the American Association of Christian Counselors, Donna has been providing individuals and families the hope and help they need for nearly 25 years as a North Carolina Licensed Clinical Mental Health Counselor Supervisor (LCMHCS) and Board Certified Professional Christian Counselor (BCPCC). She is EDIT Certified (Eating Disorder Intuitive Therapy) and has a Certificate of Completion from EMDRIA in Basic EMDR (Eye Movement Desensitization and Reprocessing Therapy).

Donna's most recent books are Silencing Insecurity: Believing God's Truth about You and Becoming Resilient: How to Move through Suffering and Come Back Stronger, both published by Baker/Revell Publishing.

Donna has been married to her husband, Mark, for 28 years, and has four miracle boys. She grew up in the Eastern part of North Carolina, met her husband in undergrad at North Carolina State University, and moved back to his hometown in Hendersonville, North Carolina 25 years ago. She loves spending time with friends and family, pulling for the Wolfpack, and hiking the beautiful mountains of Western North Carolina.

Follow Donna's author page at **facebook.com/DonnaGibbsResilience** for encouragement and updates regarding events and speaking engagements.

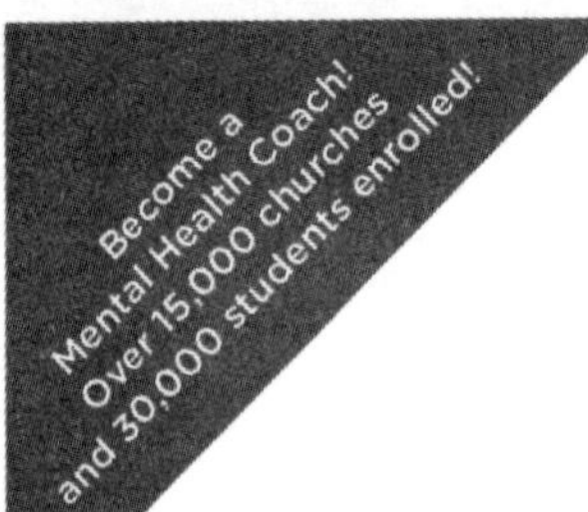

CERTIFIED

Mental Health Coach

FIRST RESPONDER TRAINING

LIMITED TIME SCHOLARSHIP

No cost to the church and tuition is FREE for students!
(One-time $54 tech support fee applies)

"Without question, this training will be one of the most, if not the most, significant projects we have ever done in the history of the AACC. We need an army of helpers in the local church—those of whom God has given natural gifts and talents to offer help, hope, and guidance to the hurting!"

Dr. Tim Clinton, President
American Association of Christian Counselors

Introducing the **Mental Health Coach Training**, a 42-hour, biblically-based training that consists of three courses. Enroll and successfully complete all three courses and become a **"Certified Mental Health Coach"** by the International Board of Christian Care.

Our 2023 mission is to engage, educate and equip an additional 6,500 churches and congregations and to train 45,000 students all over America and around the world.

Who can enroll? Under the discretion of your church, **anyone with a calling to offer help, hope, and encouragement** to those who are hurting and looking for guidance and direction in everyday life.

- 42-hour, Biblically-based, clinically-excellent training program
- Featuring some of the world's leading mental health and ministry experts
- Study anywhere, anytime, at your own pace, on any of your favorite devices!
- On-demand video lectures—No schedules!
- Available 24/7/365
- And you have one year to complete your course

Learn to help those who struggle with **Serious Mental Illness (SMI),** including topics like:

- Addiction
- Trauma and Abuse
- Grief and Loss
- Boundaries
- Panic Disorders
- PTSD
- Phobias
- Suicide
- Crisis Intervention
- Depression
- Stress and Anxiety
  ... and more!

LIGHTUNIVERSITY.COM/MENTALHEALTHCOACH

LIGHT UNIVERSITY

A Global Leader in Certificate and Diploma-Based Education

The Leader in Certificate and Diploma Based Christian Counseling Education

5 SCHOOLS OF STUDY & OVER **200 COURSES** TO CHOOSE FROM!

BIBLICAL COUNSELING

Gain crucial knowledge necessary to help others with confidence using the Bible and the latest counseling wisdom and insights.

LIFE COACHING

Make a difference in the lives of your clients by integrating sound biblical principles with relevant life coaching materials and professional practice.

CRISIS RESPONSE

Provide immediate assitance to emergency and disaster relief agencies with effective Christian leadership and biblically-based principles.

MARRIAGE AND FAMILY

Help clients preserve and promote the institution of marriage, family and the biblical principles on which they are based.

MENTAL HEALTH COACHING

Help clients obtain and maintain stability, manage difficult symptoms, rebuild relationships, and find a purpose for living.

CONTINUING EDUCATION

Browse our extensive course catalog for continuing education credits or your professional counseling license.

Visit the **all-new LightUniversity.com** website, featuring **new and improved search capabilities, course bundling options,** and more!

1-800-526-8673 • ADMISSIONS@LIGHTUNIVERSITY.COM